GENOCIDE

The Psychology of Mass Murder

Peter du Preez

BRIEFINGS
Series Editor: Peter Collins

BOYARS/BOWERDEAN
LONDON. NEW YORK

First published in 1994 jointly by
the Bowerdean Publishing Co. Ltd., 8 Abbotstone Rd, London SW15 1QR
and Marion Boyars Publishers, 24 Lacy Rd., London SW15 1NL
and 237 East 39th St., New York, NY 10016

Distributed in Australia and New Zealand by
Peribo Pty Ltd, Terrey Hills, NSW 2084

© Peter du Preez 1994

The **BRIEFINGS** series is the property of
the Bowerdean Publishing Co. Ltd.

A CIP catalogue record for this book is available from the British Library.
A CIP catalog record for this book is available from the Library of Congress.

ISBN 0 7145 2977 - X Original Paperback

Designed and typeset by Bowerdean Publishing Co. Ltd.
Printed and bound in Great Britain by Itchen Printers Ltd., Southampton.

CONTENTS

Introduction

Chapter 1   The Puzzle of Genocide   1

Chapter 2   Genocides of Colonization and
             Decolonization   13

Chapter 3   Purifying the Nation   28

Chapter 4   Politicide   48

Chapter 5   Explaining Genocide   65

Chapter 6   The Social Psychology of Genocide   86

Chapter 7   Psychodynamics and Ideological
             Transformation   103

Chapter 8   The Future of Genocide   122

             Bibliography   136

             Index   144

BRIEFINGS is a new series of short books to explain and clarify complex contemporary subjects, written for the non-specialist by experts in their fields. Themes and topics covered will include Feminism, Education, Cosmology, Medical Ethics, Political Ideology, Structuralism, Quantum Physics and Comparative Religion among others.

INTRODUCTION

Until recently most people thought of genocide as a phenomenon to be located in the past. History has been periodically disfigured by the systematic slaughter of whole categories of human beings in order to exterminate, in its entirety, the group to which they belonged. Most commonly, in the past this has been a matter of the adherents of one religious group seeking to massacre the men, women and children of another. However, crusades, wars of religion, inquisitions and other supposedly sacred persecutions are now seen as barbaric and are acknowledged as a source of terrible shame by contemporary adherents of the religious faiths concerned.

In modern times the best known and most comprehensive attempt at genocide has been the Nazi holocaust which has come to be seen as the supreme manifestation of the capacity of human beings to do evil.

Nevertheless, the very appallingness of the Nazi treatment of the Jews was so self-evident that it came to appear inconceivable, after Nazism had been defeated in the Second World War, that such genocidal policies could ever again be adopted and pursued. Certainly, fascism as a serious and openly avowed political creed was utterly discredited, and it took only a little longer for racism in all its forms to be accounted an unequivocal political evil. This reinforced the impression that the world would never again tolerate the official killing by governments of vast numbers of defenceless people whose only crime was their membership of some politically unpopular group.

i

The extent to which Stalin had practised genocide prior to the Second World War only became clear later and more slowly. In terms of sheer numbers Stalin's slaughter of the kulaks was even more devastating than Hitler's genocide, but Stalin — and his apologists — were in a better position both to conceal the extent of the killings and to represent their victims as enemies of the revolution or at least obstacles to essential economic progress. Even when the truly genocidal character of Stalin's terror became known, this did not seriously disturb the belief that genocide must now be a thing of the past. After all, this had occurred in the 1920s and 30s and in the chaotic aftermath of revolution and civil war. This comforting and, indeed, complacent conviction that genocide is a phenomenon which need no longer concern us has recently become untenable. There are at least two decisive and interrelated reasons for this.

The first is the resurgence of antique ethnic hatreds in the aftermath of the collapse of the communist hegemony in the erstwhile Soviet bloc. This has re-legitimised potentially genocidal policies in this part of the world and, most notoriously of course, in former Yugoslavia where a policy of "ethnic cleansing" against Muslims has been openly adopted and brutally pursued. Nor is it possible to regard circumstances in ex-Yugoslavia as unique. Throughout the former Soviet Union, ethnic conflict is rife and has the potential to issue in genocide.

The second main reason why we now need to concern ourselves with genocide as a possible reality in global politics has to do with the much greater (media-induced) awareness which we now have of the incidence of genocide in contemporary Africa, Asia and South America.

Until very recently, the reality for better or for worse was that atrocities, including genocidal atrocities, in these parts of the world were little known outside the countries in which they occurred. As such, they impacted neither on public opinion, nor on political leadership especially in the West which was, in any case, overwhelmingly preoccupied with the problems of the Cold War.

Now, by contrast, we know much more and much more distressingly about the plight of the indigenous peoples in the rainforests of South America, of class enemies under communist regimes in Asia, of minority tribes in Africa. Moreover, the old assumption that these were matters of purely domestic politics and therefore beyond the jurisdiction of international law is eroding. This is not because international law has changed but because electorates in the West have become much more disposed to feel that their leaders should be doing something to put a stop to moral atrocities committed by foreign governments against their own subjects. And this is and will remain especially true of genocidal atrocities.

We are compelled then to see genocide as a live issue. As such, it is important for us to try to understand the nature and history of genocide and genocides, which we can only do by looking to past experience. On the other hand, if we are to gain the kind of understanding which may assist us in anticipating and controlling the future of genocide, we must also engage in theoretical speculation about the social and psychological circumstances which foster the emergence of genocidal politics. In this respect the conclusion of this short book is alarming. For, contrary to what has usually been assumed, the evidence suggests that genocide, far from being a freak occurrence, is a psychologically intelligible and, to that extent 'normal' response to a particular kind of social and political crisis. And if this is so, we can expect genocides to prove a recurring phenomenon unless and until we can devise strategies for neutralizing the conditions which provoke it.

Our contemporary society, though geared to discover the facts, is less well equipped to consider what such strategies must be. It is more than enough to try to address the question: "Why do genocides occur?" One thing seems certain about the possibility of preventing future genocides. This is that a necessary condition for addressing the issue both domestically and internationally will be widespread awareness of the phenomenon amongst ordinary people for whom genocidal passion is literally unimaginable. This is especially true of the ordinary people who make up the electorates in those powerful countries on whom the future of the international order now mainly depends.

CHAPTER ONE

THE PUZZLE OF GENOCIDE

The puzzle of genocide is this: Why should one category of apparently rational human beings attempt to annihilate all members of another category — men, women and children — even when the victims can offer little resistance and the act of destruction is very costly? When we examine different kinds of genocide we are able to pick out some that are more "rational" than others, in the sense that they have brought some advantage to the perpetrators; but why choose genocide when the same result could have been achieved as easily in some other way? For it is rare to find instances where the killers glory in their ruthlessness. On the contrary, in almost every case ruthlessness is disguised as a stern duty undertaken with reluctance only by the noblest and the best.

Here I shall look at one rational genocide, in which the perpetrators do obtain advantage, and at one clearly irrational genocide where the perpetrators lose more than they gain. At the same time we may consider whether these genocides differ from each other in any significant way. The genocides I shall compare are the genocide of the Herero in what was South West Africa and is now Namibia and the genocide of the Jews in Nazi Germany. Here I shall examine the two examples in the barest possible way to make the distinction between rational and irrational genocide. In later chapters each will be more fully presented.

Germany became a colonizing power late in comparison with its European neighbours. In 1892 the first German colonists arrived in South West Africa; railroads were driven through the country to make the settlement of cattle ranchers possible, and the process of dispossession of the indigenous people began. This dispossession is an integral part of the process of colonization and it continues today. (An example is East Timor, where the Indonesian government, which wishes to dispossess the East Timorese, has already slaughtered 200,000 of them.) By 1903, a mere 11 years after the arrival of the first colonists, it was proposed that the Hereros should be moved into reservations for their own protection. Railroads were to be driven right into the heart of Herero country, and the grazing and water rights on either side of the railroad would be annexed (as had already been done wherever railroads were built in the colony).

At this stage the Herero, realizing that their own lands were about to be expropriated, rebelled. The Germans, under the command of General Lothar von Trotha, embarked upon a war of extermination against them, reducing their numbers from about 80,000 in 1904 to 14,000 by 1911. The explicit intention of von Trotha's campaign was to "remove" the Herero from the country altogether. (In our more detailed account of the Herero war we shall note a dispute between two authorities on the precise meaning of von Trotha's words.)

Isn't this perfectly rational? It may be disgusting, horrible, vile and immoral, but it is surely rational to eliminate those who resist dispossession. The policy of extermination cleared the way for the colonists. It entitled them, under the fundamental principles of colonization — "right of discovery" and the "right to vacant land" — to occupy the land so vacated. This they proceeded to do. The advantage was clear; the legality was hardly disputed, given the ample precedent of four centuries; and duty called. Christians were taking over from savages. Civilization was replacing barbarism. Does this genocide really need an explanation? Within the European tradition of colonization, its rationale was unexceptionable, however rough.

We now look at an example of genocide which shocks us because of its scale and irrationality. This is the Nazi genocide of over five million Jews and other groups, such as the 200,000 gypsies. What is puzzling about this — when we try to analyze it in terms of benefit to the perpetrators — is the costliness of the process. Germany lost brilliant scientists, inventive entrepreneurs, skilled workers, and millions of ordinary, loyal citizens who would undoubtedly have supported the German war effort. Enormous resources were devoted to the task of killing Jews and others, even when it was clear that the war was being lost. The aim was to make Europe free of Jews. Why? Because, as is apparent from Nazi propaganda, the mere existence of Jews was a threat to the racial purity and soul of the Aryan race. Jews were, in fact, non-humans or, worse still, anti-humans.

Looked at from their own perverted standpoint, it is possible to argue that it was perfectly rational of the Nazis to exterminate Jews and that, on grounds of rationality alone, there is no distinction between the extermination of the Herero and that of the Jews. Both are "rational" in the sense that they involve means–end calculations; they attempt to achieve goals by the most direct means available. Their success or failure is immaterial, since many perfectly rational endeavours fail. Given such an empty definition of rationality this may indeed be so. The difference is one of profitability, not of rationality. People do many unprofitable things such as attempting to understand the universe, painting pictures, building cathedrals or exploring outer space and we do not therefore think them irrational.

We should therefore attempt a more penetrating analysis of genocide. Mere profitability is an inadequate criterion to distinguish it from other activities. We need to know: How is a point reached where genocide seems to be a possible or even a desirable course of action? Given the many ways of solving problems, why choose this particular solution? How does killing come to seem reasonable? What are the premises, the forms of reasoning and the experiences which lead to genocide? How do we reach the stage of planning the extermination of a whole people?

There is a "rationality of genocide" just as there is a rationality of business or athletics or war or science. These forms of rationality — talk, skills, strategies, model solutions, premises, general assumptions, methods of training — have a history. They are activities within which problems are constituted and solutions are found. In exactly this way, genocidal solutions do not arise out of nothing. We can usually trace their history and their evolving forms. The process of genocide, if it is to be sustained, must be practised and perfected. The distinction between the perpetrators and their victims must be given a significant form — a sacred or scientific basis. The necessity of the task must be spelled out for everyone to understand. The methods must be designed so that they are appropriate to the local culture of law and order, or to the circumstances of killing. Genocide must become a solemn duty. The term "rationality" is explanatory only when referring to options within a practice or an ideology. Only then can we evaluate the skill with which one means rather than another is selected.

The puzzle of genocide becomes, therefore:

How does a pattern of talk and action arise in which genocide seems a rational option?

What I propose to do is to look at some facts and figures. How common is genocide? What are some of its characteristics? How have various people tried to define genocide? Once we have done this we can turn to explanations.

How common is Genocide?

Let us examine some genocides and see what they have in common. As a working definition we start with something very broad. We state that genocide is the deliberate killing of people primarily because they are categorized as being of a certain kind, with certain attributes.

The first thing to note is that genocide is not new. We read in the Old Testament: "Now go and smite Amalek, and utterly destroy all that they have, and spare them not, but slay both man and woman, infant and suckling, ox and sheep, camel and ass" (1 Samuel, 15:3). Those who have written on the subject draw our attention to the genocides of Genghis Khan (only wolves and ravens survived his passage), Tamerlane (who built 20 towers of skulls in Syria in 1400 and 1401 AD), the Crusades (almost all of which started with pogroms against the Jews and ended — when triumphant — with massacres of Muslims), and the religious wars of the Reformation. In addition there were the processes of colonization, already touched on, in which many indigenous peoples disappeared. An example from the history of European colonization would be the annihilation of the Pequots by the early settlers on the east coast of the United States.

It is not difficult to guess that genocides were fairly common in antiquity, given that peoples and empires disappeared abruptly, that religions often commanded the genocide of enemies, and that city was built upon destroyed city (Chalk and Jonassohn, 1990).

Have we advanced beyond genocide in the twentieth century? The record confirms our worst fears. It is difficult to see any evidence of progress in the elimination of the various forms of political violence, ranging from torture to terrorism, war and genocide. A list of some of the most notable genocides of the twentieth century is given below, but I fear that many genocides and genocidal massacres have been omitted, among them genocides in Ethiopia, Somalia, the Congo, the Sudan, the rain-forests of Brazil, Nicaragua and Peru, and the current war in what was Yugoslavia, where attempts are being made to create ethnically "pure" regions by killing or driving off those who do not fit in. Many more cases are given in Chapter 5. In the list below each genocide is identified by the name of its victims.

HERERO (1904): annihilated by German army under Lothar von Trotha. About 64,000 died in a total population of 80,000. The ideological warrant was the assumed right of European powers to colonize primitive and uninhabited lands.

ARMENIANS (1915): annihilated by Turkish government assisted by "spontaneous" action of the population. Between 600,000 and 1,000,000 were killed. The ideological warrant for genocide was the redefinition of Turkey as the country of the Turks by militant Turkish nationalists. Previously it had been part of the Ottoman Empire, an empire of many peoples.

KULAKS (1929-1933), or independent peasantry: annihilated by the Soviet government. Between 14 and 15 million peasants, largely in the Ukraine, died in a state-engineered famine which was intended to break resistance to collectivization. The ideological warrant for genocide was Marxist-Leninist theory, which was used by Stalin to construe the independent peasants as class enemies.

5

JEWS (1940-1945): annihilated by the Nazis and their collaborators. Over 5 million Jews were killed. The ideological warrant for genocide was national socialism, which defined Jews as a threat to the racial purity of Germans and other "Aryans".

GYPSIES (1940-1945): annihilated by the Nazis as part of their racial hygiene programme. An estimated 220,000 were killed. The ideological warrant was national socialism.

TUTSI (1963): attacked by Hutu in Rwanda. Between 10,000 and 12,000 were slaughtered. The context was the withdrawal of colonial power and the consequent internal struggle for dominance.

HUTU (1972): attacked by Tutsi in Burundi. Between 100,000 and 200,000 were killed in a postcolonial struggle for domination.

INDONESIAN COMMUNISTS (1966): massacred by Indonesian government. About 500,000 were killed. The ideological warrant was a "holy war" by Muslims and some Christians against atheistic communists and foreigners.

IBO (1966): attacked by Hausa-dominated Nigerian government forces. Between 600,000 and 1,000,000 died. The ideological warrant was the right of the state to prevent secession.

BENGALI (1971): attacked by Pakistani government forces in Bangladesh. About 3 million died, 2 million were left homeless, and 10 million became refugees. The ideological warrant was the right of the state to prevent secession.

CLASS ENEMIES (1966-1976): persecuted by Chinese state during the Cultural Revolution, resulting in an unknown number of deaths. The ideological warrant was a Maoist version of communism.

BOURGEOISIE (1975-1978): killed by Khmer Rouge in Kampuchea. Between 1 and 2 million deaths in a total population of about 7 million. The ideological warrant was militant communism and an attempt to eliminate all those who were contaminated by westernization.

TIMORESE (1975-Present): attacked in East Timor by the Indonesian army. About 200,000 killed in an attempt to colonize East Timor. The ideological warrant is the unification of the Indonesian state, as well as the various assumptions of superiority which accompany colonization.

We could multiply examples. During the partition of India after the British withdrawal in 1947, Muslim and Hindu attacked each other and between 200,000 and 500,000 were killed. After the defeat of Yugoslavia by the Axis powers in the Second World War, Croats seized the opportunity to kill "hundreds of thousands" of Serbs, who had dominated up to then.

Examples of genocide, genocidal massacre and massacre shade into each other and it is often difficult to arrive at any estimate of the numbers killed, since there are no accurate before and after census figures. All that we can establish is that the massacre of unarmed and helpless people is a common feature of recent history.

Now that we have given several examples of genocide and near-genocide, let us turn to definitions. What distinguishes genocide from other forms of killing on a large scale? Is there a distinction, or are massacre and genocide difficult to tell apart?

What is Genocide? Some definitions

Because of its political significance, let us start this discussion by looking at the definition of genocide in the United Nations Convention on Genocide, Article II, as adopted on 9 December 1948. The term itself was first used by the jurist Raphael Lemkin in 1944 and appears in the indictment of Nazi war criminals at Nuremberg in 1945.

Article II of the UN Convention on Genocide

In the present Convention, genocide means any of the following acts committed with intent to destroy, in whole or in part, a national ethnical, racial or religious group, as such:

    a)   Killing members of the group;

    b)   Causing serious bodily or mental harm to the group;

    c)   Deliberately inflicting on the group conditions of life calculated to bring about its physical destruction in whole or in part;

    d)   Imposing measures to prevent births within the group;

    e)   Forcibly transferring children from one group to another group.

Those of us who are not lawyers may find this impressive until we study the record. The first difficulty is that there is nothing to prevent the destruction of "political" groups. In this way virtually every assault on a group may be passed off as a defence against a political movement. Hence the state has not killed members of a "group" as defined in the Convention. This would cover the mass slaughter of kulaks in Stalinist Russia, of communists in Indonesia, of "bourgeoisie" by the Khmer Rouge, or of Ibo killed in the Nigerian civil war.

There are other words in the Convention which may seem harmless to the non-lawyer but which are useful to states defending themselves against prosecution. This should not surprise us, since the Convention was drawn up by the states themselves, each very conscious of its own particular offences. The particular words are "intent" and "as such". These have been crucial to the defence of several governments. Paraguay (charged with the genocide of Guyaki Indians), Brazil (charged with the genocide of Indians of the Amazon forests), the United States (charged with committing genocide in Vietnam, Laos and Kampuchea), and Pakistan (charged with genocide in Bangladesh) have all been able to argue that there was no intent to kill the members of any group as such.

Undoubtedly, intent must be central in the clearest cases of

8

genocide. But how do we succeed in pinning legal responsibility on a government? A cynical defence (and one which has been successfully used by Paraguay in defence of its treatment of the Ache Indians) is that there may be a victim and there may be a victimizer, but there is no genocide in the absence of an intent to destroy a group (Kuper, 1981). Violence at the frontiers of rapidly expanding societies has been the cause of the elimination of many groups. Chalk argues that "the rulers of these nations are powerful and educated people who understand the inevitable consequences of their actions. When they tolerate a development process that annihilates native peoples, they are the major per- petrators of genocide" (Chalk, 1989, p.154).

Yet "process" can undermine "intent". Governments may argue that attempts to control "process" are often beyond them. They may wish to control population growth and stimulate the econ- omy and yet fail because they use incorrect methods. Consider economic relations between the developed and the developing world. These economic relations are said to result in poverty, underdevelopment and starvation. Is the developed world geno- cidal? Are the consequences inadvertent? Does anyone know how to manage the complex processes which would produce uni- versal prosperity, given the fact that there are many agents with conflicting aims? Finally, can we say that there is an attempt to define and annihilate a specific group?

CLASSES OF VIOLENT CONFLICTS

	RESISTANCE	
	YES	**NO**
SMALL	skirmish	massacre
SCALE		
LARGE	war	genocide

What we see is a range of cases, from those which are clearly genocidal to those which are violent but not genocidal. The table above makes some of the distinctions though it is not exhaustive. In war, non-combatants are spared unless they impede the conduct of war; in genocides (and genocidal massacres), there is no distinction between killing combatants and non-combatants. The prototypical case of genocide is one in which political leaders spell out their intention to eliminate a group of people. What distinguishes this from normal warfare is the thoroughness of the intention and the fact that no one will be spared. Leaders usually "normalize" genocidal intent by placing it in the framework of a general political ideology which will justify and rationalize their acts. National socialism, Marxist-Leninist communism, or militant nationalism might be the ideological framework. The intent would be spelled out by leaders in documents for secret consumption by state officials, in speeches, or in after-dinner conversations with intimates.

These would be the clear cases. There will also be a range of cases in which we might argue that the genocidal consequences of policy should have been anticipated; but there is no clear evidence that genocide was the intention. We might detect cynicism, a selfish indifference to other people, or even a malicious intention to suppress their interests. Racist policies are of this kind, with apartheid being a prime example. It resulted in the oppression of millions of people and in the mass removals of between three and four million from their homes. By impoverishing entire classes it caused the deaths of unknown numbers of adults and children due to malnutrition. It caused millions to lead lives of frustration and despair. It was a crime against humanity — but was it genocide, given that ethnic identity and the setting up of ethnic states were the basis of government? To this the reply must be that the setting up of ethnic states was a cynical attempt to camouflage naked domination. The states were too small and too poor to support the people who were forced to live in them. The sincerity of the National Party's attachment to the ethnic formula went only as far as an attachment to its own interests. Yet there has never been any evidence of a deliberate plot to exterminate any group of people. If we wish to use "genocide" with precision we cannot define it only by its consequences, just as we cannot define all acts which result in the death of a person or persons as murder. A murderer is a person who kills another person with malice aforethought. The murderer does not kill accidentally or in self defence. Murder is malicious and intentional killing against the law. Similarly, genocide is not inadvertent or incidental to other acts. It is the deliberate and intended killing of a category of persons. What does differ from case to case is the reason for the killing, just as in murder, and this will determine its scale and duration. If genocide has a clear economic or political purpose, then it will continue until that purpose is achieved. If genocide has a transcendental purpose, then it will continue until all members of a category have been eliminated or until the perpetrators have been arrested. In order to explain the differences it will probably not be necessary to resort to pathology; all that is necessary is to consider the ways in which participants construe the situation.

An example may clarify the difference between limited and transcendental genocide. If a particular group of people occupy land which settlers desire, or if a particular group of people pose a political threat, they may be killed. We may think of the German killing of the Herero in South West Africa (or any number of killings by colonizers), or of the killing of Ibo in the Biafran war to prevent their secession from the Nigerian Federation. These kinds of killings shade into "normal" warfare. Transcendental genocide, on the other hand, is based on theories of the absolute need to eliminate all members of a category, because of their intractable vileness, wickedness, dangerousness, or opposition. Religious theory of a certain kind might impose the duty of eliminating all heretics; communist theory of a kind might lead to the elimination of all capitalists; and Nazi theory demanded the elimination of all Jews and many other "impurities" from the nation. What is transcendent about these forms of genocide is that they are based on absolutes and do not cease until these absolutes have changed or the perpetrators have been defeated. They are not mere means-end murders. The elimination of the victim is the end which is sought, because the victim embodies the evil which must be removed from the world.

When we are thinking how to prevent genocide, it is important to be clear about the nature of the act. If the purpose is limited, it might be possible to prevent genocide by addressing its goals.

Political security might be achieved, for example, without the killing of large numbers of people. Economic progress might be achieved without the displacement and elimination of indigenous peoples. These are difficult problems, but we might make some progress by focusing on the goals of the killers. On the other hand, we cannot halt transcendental genocide by addressing the ends which are achieved by genocide. The end is genocide. A fundamental change of world-view is necessary before any change can be achieved. In many cases we will find that we can think of no way of preventing genocide, whether limited or transcendent, which does not require the use of force. It is difficult to imagine fruitful collaboration with deliberate mass murderers. Any assistance given to them is likely to facilitate murder.

Statesmen often have to reach decisions on questions of this kind. First they must identify the kind of threat they are facing and having done so, they then have to decide on a strategy for dealing with it. Should Saddam Hussein have been given American aid in the 1980s, even for the purpose of confronting Iran? Would negotiating with Hitler have enabled more Jews to escape the Holocaust, given that the Nazis were prepared to allow Jews to emigrate if they were paid enough for them and that they had established relations with Zionists in Israel for this purpose? Eichmann was proud of his cordial expertise in arranging such matters (Arendt, 1963). Would confrontation not have been better? There is no clear answer, even in retrospect. Certainly at the time, there was none. The Holocaust was yet to come.

Our next task is to present some case histories of the genocidal process. If we are to attempt any kind of explanation, we should review a number of examples of what it is that we are attempting to explain. In this way we may hope to identify the main problems. It will ensure, at any rate, that our explanations are offered within some kind of context.

CHAPTER TWO

GENOCIDES OF COLONIZATION AND DECOLONIZATION

Genocides occur under different circumstances, involving people of different cultures. Do they have anything in common? Isn't a general theory of genocide as unlikely as a general theory of murder and, if so, what can be learnt from studying a variety of cases?

The first possibility is that we may learn which societies are "at risk". We may find that societies in which genocides are likely to occur display specific features, such as a long history of inter-ethnic conflict or a rapid change in the relative position of social classes. We will usually speculate on the causal relation between such warning signs and genocide, but this will not necessarily lead to a general theory.

Before we burden ourselves with too much speculation, it will be useful to equip ourselves with some examples. In constructing these examples we shall undoubtedly be guided by assumptions about what is significant and what is not, what led to what, and what the connections are; but there are some advantages to keeping these assumptions to a minimum. The principal advantage is that readers may feel relatively free to form their own hypotheses.

The cases we shall attempt to study are drawn from the list in Chapter 1. There are many more possibilities, but these represent a wide enough range. Now we shall have to decide how to group them. This is, of course, a preliminary hypothesis about the nature of these genocides, but we must have some way of thinking about them. The grouping is as follows:-

    1. Genocides of colonization: *Herero*
    2. Genocides of decolonization: *Ibo*
    3. Genocides of purification: *the elimination of ethnic minorities such as Armenians, gypsies, Jews and class enemies such as kulaks and the bourgeoisie.*

This organization already predisposes us to notice certain facts and ignore others.

Then we shall have to organize our histories of genocides in ways which enable us to compare them. Here we need some elementary theory of the sequence of events which leads to genocide. The theory which will be used to build these stories is so simple that we might be tempted to regard it as no theory at all. Nevertheless our hypothesis is that genocides have the following stages:-

    1. Preparation
    2. Justification
    3. Precipitation
    4. Massacre

This is very simple, but it does direct our attention in well-defined ways. What we are saying is that genocides have a history, perhaps a long history, predating the actual genocidal massacre or massacres and that we should study that history to understand why particular victims are chosen by particular perpetrators. We are also saying that we should study the justifications. Perhaps the justifications for genocide are different from justifications for other political acts. Or perhaps they are similar. After all, perfectly sane scientists and politicians have built weapons to destroy the earth. When our fear of the enemy is great enough we see no reason why we should not include total destruction in our calculations. There is a difference between an instrumental use of the fear of genocide and genocide itself. In the one case, genocide is an instrument of policy, an ultimate threat; and in the other case, it is the object of the policy. Are there such cases? Finally, our narrative structure leads us to attend to precipitating events. Are they necessary? Do they have anything in common? We now proceed to our first case, the Herero.

Genocides of colonization - The Herero of Namibia

Preparation

We should understand the massacre of the Herero as coming near the end of a long process of European colonization, in which theory and practice were established. There were local variants and degrees of brutality and dispossession, but the fundamental principles of "right of discovery" and "unoccupied land" were widely accepted. The major political problems of sharing out territory were negotiated with other European powers.

From the fifteenth century onwards Europeans — particularly Portuguese, Spanish, Dutch, French and English — began to colonize the globe. They went in search of adventure, trade, gold, land and souls. To many of us, the pursuit of souls may seem mysterious. Why should anyone wish to convert anyone else? Then we may remember the ideological struggles of our own time and the importance which is attached to political faith. To convert others is to confirm the truth of one's faith and to build its power. The quest for souls is by no means over. In fact, as we read the records, we may begin to suspect that the quest for souls is the most important task of statecraft. It is the burden which secular ideology has inherited from religion. Something must be sacred. If it is not to be found in the next world then it is to be found in this world. Hence the astonishing spectacle of sacred politics in a secular age. Hence the sacred monsters of communism, fascism, national socialism and even capitalism. Hence the tortures and confessions. Hence the search not merely for outward compliance but for inward assent. Sacred being is always injured by dissent and enraged by non-conformism and only the sceptic can tolerate the unprincipled variety of multi-party democracy and the plural society.

No such scruples troubled the majority of the early colonizers. Soldiers followed traders, missionaries followed soldiers. There were eccentrics who found the ways of the natives interesting and even admirable; but as tensions inevitably grew, the distinctions between heathen and Christian, savage and civilized, white and coloured, became sharper and more clear cut. The detailed picture shows attempts to stem the tide of settlers, to draw boundaries, to establish reservations, and to recall governors who ill-treated indigenous peoples. Columbus was transported back to Spain in irons for ill-treating the natives of Hispaniola, but the interests which drove the process of colonization were too strong for it to be held up for long.

What accounted for the rapid spread of the Europeans and the broken resistance of the indigenous peoples? The first and most obvious factor is superior technology. This enabled the colonizers to produce superior weapons and seductive goods of trade. The second factor was organization. Because of the hierarchical and centralized organization of European states over comparatively large territories, they were able to draw on large resources and apply them where necessary, even if the application was slow by modern standards. Years might pass before decisive force could be brought to bear at a particular point, but brought to bear it was, time and again, in the conquest of colonies. In this way early defeat was converted into later victory. The third factor was ideology. Europeans were convinced of their moral superiority. The humblest among them was a Christian among heathen. Even if the natives had converted to Christianity they were still barbarians. The fourth factor was often disease. In many parts of the world, contact with Europeans led to disastrous epidemics among the indigenous peoples. Up to three-quarters of the native inhabitants of what was later called New England died of disease after the visit of an English fishing fleet in 1616. The Pilgrims who arrived in 1620 found a land which had been depopulated. Measles and smallpox played a similar role in many parts of the world.

Finally, two important doctrines rationalized conquest and occupation. These were the "right of discovery" — or the right of Christians to displace heathen and savage; and the doctrine of "unoccupied land", which held that land which was not owned by anyone in particular was not owned by anyone at all. Thus, communal hunting grounds were not property in the European sense. Unoccupied land was forfeit to those who could make civilized use of it. These principles still rationalize the destruction of the rain-forests and the dispossession of the indigenous Indians.

We now turn from these general comments to the particulars of the massacre of the Herero.

Germany, as already noted, was a latecomer in the process of colonization. Portuguese, Spanish, British, French and Belgians either had or were busy acquiring vast territories. It was in early 1892 that the first German settlers arrived in South West Africa. By that time, they knew exactly how they should behave. They had come as civilized people to a land of savages. The doctrines of "right of discovery" and "unoccupied land" were taken for granted. Practical men of affairs knew that the natives had to be dispossessed by force or trickery, with all the solemnity of due process of law.

The theory of colonization, clearly established by long tradition, was applied to the local case. Four-and-a-half thousand colonists had arrived by 1904, when the Herero revolt began. But before 1904 railroads were driven into the country to open the way for cattle ranchers. In the process, much of the best cattle country was appropriated, or "legally" stolen from the natives. Treaties of "protection and friendship" were signed as part of the process of theft. There were clashes in which the colonists showed little respect for those they were supposed to befriend and protect. Whites accused of raping and assaulting natives were rarely convicted.

Inevitably, as the colonists occupied more and more of the best land, the scene was set for bloody resistance.

Justification

The justification of dispossession arises naturally out of the tradition of colonization, a tradition which had matured over several centuries. The Germans inherited this tradition and began participating at a time of bloated nationalism. European nations

17

began to take themselves and their national destinies very seriously towards the end of the nineteenth century. In particular, Europeans began to talk of their mission and their "racial" destiny, meaning by this their destiny as "whites" in the context of "non-whites", or as Germans, English, French and so forth in the context of other European nationals. So competing nationalisms led to ever bloodier wars to see who was top dog and to greater intolerance towards any kind of resistance to the nation and its destiny.

A wonderfully eloquent version of the European mission was produced by Ruskin at his inaugural lecture as Slade Professor of Fine Art at Oxford in 1870 when he addressed his crowded audience on the theme of Imperial Duty, and British Imperial Duty in particular; but his words expressed the European view.

> There is a duty now possible to us, the highest ever set before a nation, to be accepted or refused... . This is what England must either do or perish; she must found colonies as fast and as far as she is able, formed of her most energetic and worthiest men; seizing every piece of fruitful waste ground she can set her foot on, and there teaching these her colonists that their chief virtue is to be fidelity to their country, and their first aim is to be to advance the power of England by land and sea... (Morris, 1979, p.380).

There is also a splendidly eloquent call to men who will, for love of England, fling themselves against cannon-mouths for little pay.

An empire must be founded or the nation perish. That is the clear message in a world in which other nations are founding their own empires. We notice also the expression "fruitful waste ground". This encapsulates the entire argument of empire.

Two other elements were needed for genocidal massacre to become possible. The first was the concept of total war waged against an entire population. The precedent for this had already been established in the Anglo-Boer war of 1899-1902, during which non-combatants had been interned in concentration camps, with much loss of life. The second element was a theory that the only thing the African understands is force. This kind of theory is popular among military men, but they are usually restrained from putting it into practice. Unfortunately, the general who was placed in command of the campaign against the Herero had such a theory and little to restrain him from applying it to the full.

Precipitation

As so often happens, the authorities precipitated conflict by a combination of gestures of protection and exploitation. Though nothing could be allowed to obstruct colonization, they did hope that the natives would accept it without making too much of a fuss. With this in mind they established reserves for the accommodation and protection of the natives and began with the construction of the Otavi railway line into the heartland of Herero country. The reserves showed the Herero that they were on the verge of losing their country; the railways (with a claim to 20 kilometres on either side and all water rights) showed that the settlers would exploit the best land and own the best cattle. Simultaneously, traders began to press black employees for repayment of debts (incurred as loans, or for credit at company stores) because a new statute of limitation on contracts meant that employees could no longer be forced into perpetual renewal of work contracts in order to repay what they owed. This was an attempt to remedy an abuse, but to workers it must have had the same effect as if the state were (in modern times) to attempt legislation to protect citizens from becoming hire-purchase slaves.

Samuel Maharero (1856-1923), the supreme chief of the Herero, read the writing on the wall and attempted to forge an alliance with the Nama tribe against the Germans. The Herero, with approximately 80,000 members, was the strongest tribe in the area affected by German settlement; and the Nama, with approximately 20,000 members, was the next strongest. Both were nomadic herders whose cattle grazed the land demanded by German cattle ranchers. Maherero explicitly targeted German men as the enemy and excluded all women and children, all British, missionaries and all other tribes. They were to be spared. Unfortunately for him, he was not able to draw the Nama into a simultaneous attack on the enemy. Instead they waged successive wars and were both defeated. Provoked by this dangerous assertion of rights, Berlin demanded "unconditional surrender" and the commander of the German forces, Lothar von Trotha, decided upon extermination. He had already participated in the suppression of the Wahehe uprising in East Africa in 1896 and was convinced that he understood "the African mentality". Since the only thing that this mentality would understand was force, he resorted to a policy of "unmitigated terrorism" and the shedding of "rivers of blood" (Drechsler, 1980).

Massacre

Here we come to a difference of opinion between Drechsler (1980) and Poewe (1985) about von Trotha's intention and hence the nature of the act.

The crucial battle was fought at the Waterberg in 1904. One version of the outcome is that the German forces were so deployed that the Herero could only break out by escaping into the desert. The other version is that the Herero escape was unintended and was in fact an error which would later be dressed up as a triumph of strategy. The consequence, though, was disastrous for the Herero. Once they had escaped into the desert they were driven deeper and deeper in until they died of thirst. Von Trotha's views were uncompromising, at least as they were presented to the Herero. He proclaimed that the Herero would have to leave the country and that every Herero "with or without rifle, with or without cattle" would be shot. Drechsler reads this literally, Poewe maintains that it was psychological warfare, intended to deter Herero guerrilla bands from attacking German troops. She points to the precedent of a speech in 1900 to the German China Corps, of which von Trotha had been a member. "No pardon will be given" was the phrase used, but this slogan was never followed. Another disagreement concerns von Trotha's use of the word *vernichten* which means, literally, "to annihilate". Almost as if he had read the UN Convention on Genocide and decided to make himself a prime example, he reported to the General Staff that "the nation must be destroyed as such". Yet Poewe, pointing to numerous uses of *vernichten* shows that its more general use is "to break the resistance of". According to her reading, von Trotha was attempting to break the resistance of the Herero by various means, including psychological warfare. Against the genocide theory is also the fact that collection camps were prepared for 8,000 prisoners before the Waterberg battle. Yet this is not incompatible with the destruction of prisoners, as our unfortunate experiences show us. There was also the problem of caring for refugees; von Trotha made it clear in his proclamation that he would not accept any more women and children — shots would be fired to drive them back to their people. In orders to the forces it was made clear that these shots should be fired over the heads of the women and children and that no atrocities were to be committed. The reason given for this policy was that the women and children would spread disease and overtax the resources of the German army.

The most terrible aspect of his conduct of the war was his denial of access to the water holes to all Herero, including women and children. In the desert, this was murder. At first, as Pool (1991) shows in his biography of Maharero, Berlin supported von Trotha's methods: he was congratulated by Kaiser Wilhelm II and decorated with the *Pour le Mérite.* Later, probably as a result of the efforts of the Rhenisch Missionary Society, he was instructed to avoid all atrocities and to spare lives.

The desert did von Trotha's job for him. It broke the resistance of the Herero — if that is all he intended — and more. Those Herero who had escaped the German ring of steel found themselves driven into a trap from which they were not allowed to escape. They died of thirst. The desert war reduced their numbers from about 80,000 to about 15,000. (This estimate is based on a comparison between the population in 1903 and in 1915.) After the war, the opportunity to claim tribal land was fully utilized, and those who were even remotely connected with the Herero resistance were punished by expropriation. ("Whether they carried out, or aided and abetted, warlike acts will make no difference".) The "natives will be deprived of the possibility of raising cattle" *(Report by Hans Tecklenberg, Deputy Governor SWA).*

Their numbers decimated, their organization destroyed, their best

21

lands taken, the Herero were broken. If genocide was not intended, it was nevertheless achieved.

At this stage I shall not attempt to draw any general conclusions. These will follow after all the cases have been presented. The next cases show some of the dangers of decolonization.

Genocides of decolonization — The Biafran war and the Ibo

The Biafran war (1966-1967) was waged to prevent the secession of Biafra (which was 64% Ibo at the time of the war) from the Nigerian Federation, a legacy of British imperialism. Between 600,000 and 1,000,000 Biafrans died while the UN stood by, apparently unable to intervene. The reason for the failure to intervene was that the secession of Biafra might lead to secessions in many other states which were also artificial conglomerates created by the process of colonization and now exposed to the ethnic tensions of post-independence politics. In a world of multinational or multi-ethnic states it is dangerous to admit the claims of nationalism and ethnicity. And the colonial powers were not eager to see their legacy questioned. Hence, not one of the 126 members of the UN raised the matter. Members of the Organization of African Unity (OAU) solemnly reaffirmed their adherence to the principle of respect for the sovereignty and territorial integrity of member states and condemned secession in any member state, at their meeting in Kinshasha in September 1967. What else could they do? To admit that ethnic groups should have the right to secede could have led to widespread political disintegration.

We see a similar situation in Eastern Europe today. What should be done about the claims to independence of different national groups in Yugoslavia and the former Soviet Union? And should each national group be allowed to strengthen its claims to independence by "purifying" itself, expelling foreign or unwanted elements? Outsiders are frightened of the treatment they will receive, for the simple reason that the urge to separate is often the culmination of a long struggle in which much injury has been inflicted by one group on another.

Before going on to an account of the Biafran war, we should note that it was not exceptional in the scale of civil wars. Both the Spanish Civil War and the American Civil War cost as many lives as the Biafran war did.

Preparation

The opening act of the Biafran war was the creation of Nigeria, which became the largest British colony after the amalgamation of Northern and Southern Nigeria in 1914. By the mid-twentieth century its population was 32 million. The main problem is quite simple. The peoples who inhabit Nigeria have very little in common. The north and the south belong to different language groups which attach themselves to different religions. In the north, the Hausa (the majority group), are Islamic. In the south-east, the Ibo have been converted to Christianity. Yet in spite of this, the Hausa were preferred by their colonial governors, largely because they were disciplined and easy to rule, accustomed as they were to the autocracy of the Emirs. Once the Emirs were vanquished, they could be allowed to continue to rule under the control of the Crown. This was cheap and effective. The Emirs were attached to a system which kept them in power, even if the cost was the fossilization of their domains. No missionaries (since they were Muslim) meant no dangerous education. This suited both the Emirs and the colonial government. The technology of the state was serviced by easterners (largely Ibo) who lived in segregated Strangers' Quarters. By 1966 there were 1,300,000 of them in the north. It was the easterners who had reaped the mixed benefits of modernization: missionaries, schools and technology. It was the combination of ethnic hostility and differences in the degree of modernization and hence participation in the economy that led to conflict. Northerners resented the degree to which easterners dominated the economy and the civil service; easterners resented the degree to which northerners dominated the government. Even before independence, Ibo had been attacked and killed in the north.

After independence in 1960 the power struggle commenced in earnest, with each group fearing the domination of the other. In the electoral campaign of 1964, votes were sought by alleging

23

Ibo domination in strongly racist language. Thuggery became a common feature of elections: candidates were prevented from registering and campaigning, ballot papers vanished, candidates were detained, new regulations were introduced at the last minute and only mentioned to selected candidates, and polling agents were murdered. The party which lost the elections could hardly be expected to respect the result. A military coup solved problems of law and order for a time, but in the background the old problem was ripening. Though the southerners were more competent and better educated, they were being held back from dominating the civil service, education and the judiciary by a policy of regionalization. This barrier to their advancement was threatened when General Ironsi, the military ruler of Nigeria, declared for unification. Waves of panic spread among those who feared that they would be displaced by more competent Ibo. The Ibo would run the country, having become more educated than the northerners.

Justification

It is difficult for those who live in democracies to think of an elected majority government as a radical innovation, but its introduction often sweeps away existing powers and exposes minorities to permanent domination. Equally, it enhances the power of those who are in the majority. They embrace nationalism and the legitimate dictatorship of majority government. Once the state has been created, whether it be unitary or federal, there will be strong interest in keeping it together. This interest will be supported from outside when there are many states which are similar agglomerations. The revolutionary doctrine of separate states for separate nationalities (or whatever grouping seems most significantly natural at the time) will be opposed by the equally radical doctrine of one people in three parts (or whatever the number). Each of these doctrines has violent consequences. Circumstances will dictate the degree of violence which is necessary to translate doctrine into political reality. The doctrine of separation becomes emotionally and politically compelling when one ethnic or national group fears suppression or even when economic interests are threatened (the opposition of North and South in the American Civil War is an example of the latter). The doctrine of the unitary state (or no secession) will become compelling when the seceding group is seen as walking off with important assets and betraying the ideals of the state. Even more frightening is the possibility of a chain reaction. If one national group or region is allowed to withdraw, what is to stop others from following? This was a real danger in Nigeria, where Yoruba, Hausa and Ibo were almost equally powerful rivals. Nigeria had been created. It had important common assets. Since the new rulers were not keen on having these divided and depleted, secession meant war.

Precipitation

The war was precipitated by the secession of the easterners (Biafra) in 1967, which we could trace back to the Kano massacre described below and to other attacks on easterners.

Massacre

In May 1966 massacres of easterners commenced in Kano in the northern region. What started as student demonstrations turned into a vicious attack. Armed thugs entered the Strangers' Quarters bent on pillage, rape and murder. As is usual in these kinds of attack, men, women and children were equally subjected to bloody murder. Armed thugs were conveyed in miraculously provided transport from other towns to join the carnage. A similar pattern has become familiar in present-day South Africa: The uncontrolled attack, the mysterious assistance, the bystander police.

There were several further massacres. The easterners in the north were particularly vulnerable, but their situation in Nigeria as a whole was not reassuring. They made up only 13.5 million of the total Nigerian population. It seemed that the only solution was to secede. Since there had been a great deal of secessionist talk from various parties, including northerners, easterners may have supposed that secession would be tolerated. It was not. The balance of power had changed.

The war was grossly unequal. On the one hand was an army supplied with an abundance of modern weapons; on the other, an army with Mausers and captured weapons. Towards the end, in August 1968, legend has it that "Biafran soldiers defended on two bullets a day, attacked on five" (Forsyth, 1969, p. 206). The Wilson government adopted a posture of neutrality in public, but privately supplied the Nigerian government with most of its arms. And in secret it attempted to persuade other governments not to recognize Biafra. This is hardly surprising, given that Great Britain had created the Federation of Nigeria and Biafra had spoilt the game by seceding.

The war was cruel. Biafra's cause was publicized internationally by the picture of a hunger-wracked child. But who was responsible? One view is that, within Biafra, the cities and elites continued to live relatively well and that this rather blurs the picture of Federation-imposed starvation. The other is that famine was deliberately imposed by blockade, resulting in the deaths of 300,000 children under the age of 10. Furthermore, as part of a policy of genocide, leaders of all kinds (teachers, technicians, chiefs) were killed in captured areas; and Ibo civilian dissidents were massacred in the midwest after the withdrawal of Biafran forces. There were also widespread massacres of unarmed civilians by many units of the Nigerian army. While the war was being conducted, a genocidal theme song was broadcast by government-controlled radio in the north:

> Let us go and crush them. We will pillage their property, rape their womenfolk, kill off their menfolk and leave them uselessly weeping. We will complete the pogrom in 1966.

A contrary view is that the Biafran government used the fear of genocide to keep their people fighting to the very end, long after there was any chance of victory or even stalemate. They staged the opening of a mass grave at Owerri, uncovering 300 bodies allegedly killed by the Federal forces, specifically in order to unite Biafrans by terror (De St Jorre, 1972).

Aftermath

After the war an amnesty was announced for all who had fought on the Biafran side, and the post-war genocide which many Biafrans had feared did not happen. Nor were any medals awarded for service in a war in which there could be no victors and no vanquished. Though the war had been fought with great ferocity, once the goal had been attained, there was no systematic persecution or elimination of any particular class or ethnic group. Here we see that the theory or ideology of the participants is important and should always be taken seriously in trying to predict what will happen. If a war is being fought for limited ends, then it may be bloody and cruel but it is not likely to be genocidal. Once the ends have been achieved, the killing will cease. This is quite different from a campaign to eliminate or liquidate a group of people as such. In this respect, the Nazis and communists differed from others in developing genocidal strategies. For them, there could be no end until the race or class enemy had been eliminated. The helplessness of the enemy and the inequality of the struggle made no difference.

The crucial difference is between limited and transcendent goals. Policies which are pragmatic, prudent, and limited will be pursued until the goal is achieved. Since the aims are limited, they will very rarely attempt the total elimination of a group or the total redesign of society. Political solutions are limited solutions and are not intended to solve all the problems of a society.

We can now understand why many scholars reject the idea that the Biafran war was genocidal in intent or result. It was bloody and it might have been wrong, but it was not within the scope of the UN definition of genocide, except for the 1966 massacres in Kano. These were directed against the members of a specific group primarily because of their group membership, with no one being spared in the slaughter.

CHAPTER THREE

PURIFYING THE NATION

"...we young ones had nothing to do with this old system. In the fiery breath of war we young ones fearfully realized how empty were the concepts of this system... .We young Germans of the Great War had nothing, nothing at all in common any more with the rotten world of the old system and saw it fall apart without any regret." (Gregor Strasser)

All genocides are intended to "purify" the nation, but in some the purpose of purification seems to be more obvious than in others. In such cases we often find groups which are a permanent affront to the majority, because their very existence challenges the universal validity of the beliefs of that majority. This was the misfortune of the Armenians in Turkey, of the Jews in Europe, and of heretics everywhere, particularly during periods of national insecurity or looming catastrophe. When these groups are vulnerable and enduring minorities, they are sometimes referred to as "hostage groups". But hostages are usually released when blackmail has succeeded. These groups seldom are. They are more appropriately called "sacrifice groups". They are, from time to time, sacrificed to the purity of the majority. In times of crisis and defeat there is usually a sense of betrayal and the question is asked: Who has betrayed the people? Sacrifice groups have valuable characteristics at such times. They are outsiders who have not only a different but an opposing faith, the very existence of which may easily be construed as a threat to the majority; they often have outside links with the enemy; and they have wealth and positions which leaders of the dominant group would like to redistribute to their most loyal followers. In fact, the success of the sacrifice group often "explains" the failure of the insiders. Quite obviously, the majority are poor because the outsiders are rich; the majority do not have jobs because the outsiders have taken them all, especially the best ones; and catastrophe is looming because the outsiders have betrayed the country. A government which sacrifices the outsiders shows that it is on the side of "the people", or whatever the current term is for the sacred majority. In this way, old quarrels are used to distract people from the causes of present failure. Firm action shows that the state (embodying the people) is strong and not weak. People begin to believe that they can face up to dangers which previously made them feel helpless. By smiting the weak, who have become in fantasy a threatening monster, they gain confidence. The steps in this psychological trickery can be represented as follows:

Someone is threatening us; we are weak

We are threatening someone; we are strong

When we kill those who threaten us we shall be stronger.

Fortunately this logic does not always prevail, or else there would be many more genocides than there are.

Leadership is crucial. An example is the way in which Hitler used the Jews as a sacrifice group. He wrote:
The art of leadership consists in consolidating the attention of the people against a single adversary and taking care that nothing will split this attention. (*Mein Kampf*, 1939, p.110.)

What we should do now is to look at some cases and see whether we can understand the circumstances that made the logic of genocide somehow more alluring than other possible courses of action.

Before genocides of purification we observe a process of sacralization; the killers come to believe that they are members of a sacred body and that their victims are evil. Genocide then

29

becomes a form of religious sacrifice where human life is demanded by bloodthirsty gods; the faith is different, but the desire for purification is the same. Killing is an attempt to become and defend a sacred being; and this is why genocide may be pursued contrary to the best interests of those who attempt it. I shall discuss two cases of "purification" — the attempts to eliminate the Armenians and the Jews.

The Armenians

For five days the whole convoy marched completely naked under the scorching sun. For another five days they did not have a morsel of bread, nor even a drop of water. They were scorched to death by thirst. Hundreds upon hundreds fell dead on the way, their tongues were turned to charcoal, and when, at the end of the five days, they reached a fountain, the whole convoy naturally rushed towards it. But here a policeman barred the way and forbade them to take a single drop of water. Their purpose was to sell it . (Walker, 1980, p. 220)

Preparation

The Armenians had been Christians since the fourth century AD. By the end of the fourteenth century, the Armenian kingdom had lost its independence and by the second half of the nineteenth century it was divided between Turkey and Russia. This was a deadly division for the Armenians. Not only were Turkey and Russia powerful rivals and frequent enemies, but they differed in faith. In times of war, the Christian Armenians could easily be seen as betrayers of their Islamic neighbours.

Even within the relatively tolerant Ottoman Empire there had been discrimination against the Armenians as a Christian minority. They paid special taxes and were prohibited from bearing arms; in some areas they were not allowed to speak their own language except in prayers (Hovanissian, 1986).

In the aftermath of the Russo-Turkish war of 1877-1878 the ill-effect of dividing Armenia between Russia and Turkey became evident. Armenian leaders made an understandable but ill-judged appeal to the commander of the victorious Russian forces for protection under the peace treaty. This confirmed the worst suspicions of the Turks and redoubled the venom of subsequent attacks on them. Many a struggling minority has made the same mistake and has suffered the same fate. What is more natural than to appeal for protection to a clearly victorious army? But an army is merely an instrument of policy and it often turns out that the minority is expendable in the peace treaty and is abandoned to its fate. The Kurds and Shi'ites discovered this bitter truth in Iraq in 1991 when they assumed that the UN forces were about to overthrow Saddam Hussein.

The Armenians found that they were not among the nations granted independence after the Russo-Turkish war. All that was demanded of the Turks was that they should treat the Armenians better. This was a fresh provocation. Worse was to follow. The European powers, deciding that the existence of the Ottoman Empire was a necessary check to Russian ambitions in the Mediterranean, rejected the treaty that had led to its dismemberment and bullied the Russians into an immediate withdrawal of their forces. The Sultan was to report improvements in the position of the Armenians to the European powers. But who would respond if reports were unsatisfactory? Were the Armenians important enough to upset relations with the Sultan? By forcing the Russians to withdraw without securing the position of the Armenians the European powers had already shown that they were not. The exact formula for European inaction was supplied by the Duke of Argyll: "What was everybody's business was nobody's business." In due course a series of massacres occurred: in 1894 at Sassun and in 1895 in Trebizond between 100,000 and 200,000 Armenians were killed.

In the period leading up to the First World War of 1914-1918 the Ottoman Empire decayed steadily, losing territories and suffering military defeats. Reforms, such as they were, ended in the coup by the ultra-nationalistic "Young Turks" in 1913.

We can see how these events made the Armenians even more suspect. There is the characteristic cycle of events leading to hostility: 'We harm you because we do not trust you and this gives us even less reason to trust you. If we were in your position we would be plotting and planning, so that is what you must be doing. Besides, you confirmed our worst suspicions when you appealed to our enemies for help.'

All of this supplies the emotional energy, the hatred and fear that go into genocide; but in addition a theory is required for the killing to become truly effective on a grand scale. We must know what sacred cause we are defending in order to become thoroughly vicious.

Justification

The sacred cause was that cliche of the century — the Nation. The Young Turks espoused nationalism of the virulent kind that follows a few defeats, signs of decay, and a loss of self-esteem. Before all is lost, some earnest theorists discover who has betrayed the nation and assert that the way forward is to achieve purity by sacrifice; and the first to be sacrificed will be the traitors. The formula for Turkish nationalism was simple: "The Turks are a people who speak Turkish and live in Turkey" (Lewis, 1961, p.1). A corollary was that no one else had the right to live in Turkey; that Turkey was the land of the Turks. Excellent, except that the Ottoman Empire had been a salad of different peoples living both in what the Turks liked to think of as Turkey, and in other parts of the Empire.

Turkish nationalism was shaped by competition with the rival doctrines of Ottomanism and Pan-Islam. Ottomanism was a reformed version of the old way, a belief that the Empire was legitimately composed of different peoples who could be persuaded to cooperate with each other by the introduction of reforms and the granting of rights. Unfortunately, the minorities preferred independence wherever attainable, and this more liberal policy seemed to lead directly to disintegration. Something stronger was needed. The doctrine of Pan-Islam similarly disappointed when Arabs in alliance with Britain attacked their Turkish rulers. Quite clearly, they were not prepared to submit to Turkey for the sake of Islamic unity.

What else was sacred? The mystic unity of Turkic people everywhere, whether in Russia, Central Asia, Kazan or the Crimea, became the new sacred identity, in line with the theories of so many European nationalisms of the time. Theories of "organic" nationalism rejected the concept of minority rights and individual liberties. What mattered was mystic union. Minorities were a nuisance and threatened to infect the sacred being of the nation.

The indivisible units of historical and political action were believed to be nations — not classes, dynasties, ethnic groups, or individuals. Ziya Gokalp, an influential theorist, defined "nation" in such a way as to exclude the possibility of pluralism and diversity. One language, one culture and one religion were essential to a nation. The nation is "a basic principle of moral action" and nationalism replaces "the belief in God by belief in Nation" (Heyd, cited in Chalk and Jonassohn, 1990, p. 280). The process of sacralization was accompanied by an imaginative search for heroes. Attila, Genghis Khan and Timur were resuscitated. A new concept of blind obedience to the sacred cause of the nation was invented. People who had been under threat now discovered that they were Turks and that Turks were a mystic union of like persons who could tolerate no impurities in the national being.

Precipitation

The genocide of the Armenians was brought about by a series of defeats for Turkish arms and diplomacy. Between 1905 and 1915, Turkey lost all its Balkan possessions — and Libya as well. The territory of the Empire contracted by about a third — from 1,153,000 square miles to 729,000 square miles. This is Act I of the genocide.

Act II commences with the seizure of power by the ultra-nationalistic Young Turks, the arrival of a large German military mission in Istanbul in 1913, and the signing of a secret agreement to join Germany and Austria should Russia attack them. This opportunity to defeat Russia, with German and Austro-Hungarian assistance, was too good to be missed. A Turkish empire which would include all Turks — even those at present under the Tsar — might be possible.

Act III commences with the outbreak of war and preparations by the Turks to advance into Russia through territories inhabited by Armenians. The Turkish government tried to persuade Armenian leaders to use their influence on Armenians in Russia to provoke an uprising against the Tsar. This was a trap. If the Armenians refused, they were disloyal and secretly hoping for Russian victory. If they agreed, they showed that they had powerful and potentially dangerous links with foreign Armenians. Either way, they were a danger to the Turkish government. They refused, advised the Turks not to make war, and undertook to enlist and fight as loyal citizens of the Ottoman Empire.

Act IV commences with a disastrous winter campaign in the Caucasus. In December 1914, 95,000 Turkish troops attempted to break through to Baku and the Caspian Sea. Blizzards, snow and Russian guns killed 75,000 of them within two weeks. Simultaneously, a number of Armenians in various parts of the Empire joined Russian-sponsored volunteer units or pledged opposition to the Turks. Defeat and treachery!

Massacre

Preparations for genocide began within weeks of the Russian disaster. Armenian government employees and officials were dismissed and Armenian troops serving with the army were disarmed and formed into labour battalions. The civilian population was ordered to surrender all arms. In April 1915, four months after military defeat, deportation by forced march began from villages. Armenians of all ages were marched out of their villages and exposed to attack, rape and murder on their way to internment camps which were mere barren fields. Able-bodied men were executed. The less fortunate died of thirst, starvation and exposure, if not of assault and mutilation.

To grasp the full horror, we have to imagine the sequence of events. At first able-bodied men were summoned by a proclamation which stated that they would be deported under the protection of a benevolent government. Once collected, they were marched out of town and shot or bayonetted. Some days later the old men, women and children were summoned in the same way, but theirs was not the good fortune of summary execution. They marched along pre-arranged routes until they died. Those who fell were whipped. "The soldiers who accompanied them, and the local population who were encouraged to attack them en route saw them as good for only two things: gold and rape" (Walker, 1980, pp. 202-3).

The homes vacated by the Armenians were taken over by the 750,000 Turkish refugees from lands lost during the Balkan war. The policy of exterminating Armenians had its practical side. It also explains, in part, why no one was spared. Their property was needed. However, one should not imagine that genocide is purely practical. It requires a great vision to justify a great wrong. This explains the acts of those who collaborated with Stalin; it explains the lies of the journalists such as Duranty and Fischer who denied starvation in the Ukraine (Mace, 1988); it explains the pitiless murder of men women and children by the Turks. Why not spare innocent Armenians, the American ambassador Morgenthau asked Talaat Pasha. The reply was: "Those who are innocent today might be guilty tomorrow."

How many were killed? Calculations have been attempted, and Walker shows how a figure of about 1,000,000 is arrived at, out of a total population of between 1,500,000 and 2,000,000. The range shows how approximate the calculations must be.

We now turn to another attempt to purify the state: the genocide of the Jews in Nazi Germany.

The Holocaust

"Why should not the Jews share the privations which burden the entire nation? . . . I cannot spare a communist because he is a Jew" (Hitler to Anne O'Hare McCormick in 1933).

What can be said about the Nazi genocide of the Jews that has not already been said? My only excuse for including an account here is that it would be impossible to write a book on genocide without saying something about this terrible event.

Preparation

The genocide of the Jews had been prefigured over the centuries by pogroms and persecutions of varying ferocity and destructiveness. In addition to vulgar prejudice, there was the "deep structure" of institutionalized discrimination against Jews. The right to choose where to live, to practise certain professions, to attend schools and universities, and to practise the Jewish religion was circumscribed. Many books, pamphlets and treatises demonstrated the necessity of guarding against Jewish conspiracy.

An example of anti-Jewish propaganda is the *Protocols of the Learned Elders of Zion,* the first version of which appeared in Russia in 1903. Thereafter, it spread until it became "the most widely distributed book in the world after the Bible", according to Cohn (1967). Editions appeared in most European countries by the 1920s. In both Tsarist Russia and Nazi Germany the state vigorously promoted the distribution of the *Protocols.*

What are the *Protocols*? First, they are forgeries. Secondly, they purport to be lectures by a member of the Jewish-government-behind-the-scenes showing how world domination should be achieved. The conspiracy has been progressing behind the scenes for centuries, but the time is nearly ripe. Liberals are used by the conspirators to destroy values and discredit state authority; nation is turned against nation; the masses are to be reduced to starvation; frightful diseases are to be spread; a "plutocracy of gold" is to replace the aristocracy, and Jews are to become Freemasons and penetrate all state secrets. What is the goal of all this? A Messianic Age united under Judaism and maintained by totalitarian methods: secret spies, secret police, suppression of all political liberties, and government by a Jewish sovereign. The subordination of the gentiles will be achieved by a combination of terror and efficiency. But the *Protocols* went even further. Not only did they describe the Jewish conspiracy to take over the world, they also described the ritual sacrifice of Christian babies. This is an old story and one which had surfaced repeatedly in accusations against the Jews.

This summarizes a pamphlet of about 100 pages which was taken most seriously in the 1920s and 1930s. It was only one of many which had been launched since the fourth century AD when "Church and Synagogue were competing for converts in the Hellenistic world, and when, moreover, each was struggling to win adherents from the other" (Cohn, 1967, p 21). The conspiracy allegation had been there from the beginning. What the *Protocols* did was to bring them up to date. Two conspiracy theories — Marxism and the Jewish Conspiracy Theory — were adduced to explain the fate of the ordinary man and woman in Europe in the 1920s. And of course the two theories were blended. Marxism was a Jewish theory, and international capitalism was essentially Jewish capitalism. They were arms of the same conspiracy, crushing the naive and helpless gentile. These ideas fell more into the category of some kind of 'revelation' than of literal truth. In a conversation with Hitler, Rauschning, the Nazi leader in Danzig, observed that the *Protocols* were clearly forgeries. Hitler did not care at all. Even if they were not historically true, the "intrinsic truth was all the more convincing to him" (Ibid. p. 183).

Inspired by the intrinsic truths that had been revealed to him, Hitler condemned Jews as both bolsheviks and capitalists without any sense of contradiction. Yet why should anti-Jewish propaganda have become so powerful in Germany? It was not merely the triumph of fascism or national socialism that was responsible. In Portugal, Italy and Spain, Jews were comparatively safe.

In addition to general causes, there were specific causes: events in Germany transformed the anti-semitism that was common in Europe into a policy of genocide. First and foremost there had been the defeat in the war of 1914-18, a defeat all the more terrible because it ended a period of militant and expansive nationalism. Furthermore, after defeat there had been the humiliating terms of the Versailles treaty, compelling Germany to give up its army, to surrender territory in Europe and the colonies, and to pay reparations. Then there had been hyperinflation and unemployment. People were ready to be told that they had been betrayed. Someone had to pay. But why did Germany not convert to Marxism instead of Nazism? After all, the conditions were favourable for a revolution of the working class against a discredited middle class. And there was no powerful army to crush revolution.

The answer to this question cannot be found in a general theory of revolution or genocide. It is tactical and strategic. The conditions favoured the triumph of a radical party, but theory cannot enable us to predict which radical party would triumph. The communists and the Nazis both had their street gangs and their revolutionary plans. The outcome depended on who could make the most of the situation. We shall look at the significance of leadership and the general disposition of forces.

Firstly, the moderates had failed in their attempts to provide employment and revive the economy. Their failure to restore security and German self-respect created the conditions for radicalism. Secondly, there was no Centre. Every government since 1918 had been a coalition and every government had failed. A.J.P. Taylor (1975) summarizes the situation as follows:

*The social democrats wished to preserve the Weimar Republic, but their efforts were undermined by all the other parties and by their own incompetence or perhaps the sheer complexity of events.

*The nationalists welcomed anything that discredited the Republic.

*The communists welcomed anything that discredited the social democrats.

*The Roman Catholics of the Centre had no republican principles and would negotiate with anyone to preserve Church privileges.

*The national socialists (Nazis) were intent on destroying the Weimar Republic and establishing a new Reich.

The first strategy of the Nazis was to take a series of symbolic steps to restore German self-respect. Consistently, they played upon the fantasy that Germans were the victims of a Jewish conspiracy. The marvellous thing about Jews was that they could be used to represent capitalism, bolshevism, or simply the Jewish World Conspiracy. One of the items of propaganda which emerged in the last year of the Great War was the news that American, Russian and German Jews had raised 1.5 million marks to incite a war of German against German, brother against brother. This diabolical plot was revealed just in time. Germans! the Nazis could cry, Do not fight each other! That is a Jewish plot. Fight against your real enemies, the Jews, instead. Even if many people realized that the whole story was an invention the emotional impact remained. Someone had betrayed them. The facts might not be accurate, but the intrinsic truth remained. And what could the social democrats do about it? They were licking the boots of "every French Negro-captain" (in Hitler's words), bowing and scraping to the victors of Versailles. Hitler, from the time of his earliest speeches, identified two classes of enemy. There were those who deliberately plotted against Germany and there were those, in positions of leadership, too stupid or cowardly to resist. In this way he collected the support of those who were simply against the government as well as those who were for the ideas of the Nazi Party. Fear of a common enemy was something the Nazis were extremely skilled at exploiting. "Better Hitler than communism" was the phrase which opened the way for Hitler first within Germany and then on a wider scale in Europe (Taylor, 1975, p. 525) But fear was not enough. Force without "a new spiritual doctrine" can only be a defensive measure. Nazism was to be that spiritual doctrine. (*Mein Kampf*, p.153).

This would not have been enough without concrete advantages. Hitler was very shrewd in his offer of a great army to the generals; a bulwark against communism to the capitalists and the middle classes; an opportunity to practise racial hygiene to the medical doctors and social scientists; professional advancement to those who felt that Jews were in their way; and the prospect of loot to the thugs. In addition of course, there was the promise of employment to the unemployed while revolutionary new labour laws improved the conditions of the working class with extended holidays, social clubs, the introduction of the weekend and improved medical care. Italian fascists had limited the length of the working day in 1923. They introduced the five-day week in 1935 and encouraged sporting and cultural activities long before the democracies did. The Nazis went even further, introducing holiday facilities for working class people — seaside and ski resorts, yachting and riding schools. Then there was the Volkswagen, developed as an inexpensive car for the working man in times when driving was still something of a luxury. Hundreds of thousands of working people were given a better life under the Nazis than they had ever had before. It was clear that Hitler cared. One could trust him — provided, of course, one wasn't a Jew or a bolshevik. People of all classes were attracted to the Nazi Party because they promised a stable and efficient government, sweeping away the stuffy divisions and hierarchies of the past. They promised a community of the people — a *Volksgemeinschaft* — and a mobile and modern mass society (Broszat, 1986).

Hitler's third strategy was to make it very clear that he would be an infernal nuisance if he were left out of government. He had a private army of over two million Brownshirts and the support and sympathy of a lot of people.

These were three strategies. Each on its own was important but not decisive. Together, they added up to a formidable battle plan. But the next thing was timing. The successful fighter must have superb timing — and a lot of luck. Hitler had both.

In July 1932 the Nazis obtained 37% of the vote, and Hitler was offered the Vice-Chancellorship. He would settle for nothing less than the Chancellorship, and in an act of supreme political effrontery he declined the offer. Now his luck was as important as his nerve. The other parties could not agree to form a coalition against him. They were still more opposed to each other than they were to Hitler; they failed to grasp the fact that keeping him out of power was more important than disagreeing with each other. A fresh election was called and the Nazi share of the vote declined to 33%. Yet once more Hitler stood firm. Incredibly, the other parties still could not agree to keep him out. Political intriguers such as Bruning, Schleicher and von Papen decided that the best way to control Hitler was to give him what he wanted. This is a reasonable strategy for taming a politician like-ly to observe the rules of government and stay within the bounds of decency. It is useless when attempting to tame a Hitler, a Stalin, or a Genghis Khan. Of course, it is easy to be wise with hindsight. Contemporaries see the ordinariness of the man they are dealing with. They do not see him in the light of history but in the light of everyday life; and by that light Hitler appeared ordinary enough. On 30 January 1933 he became Chancellor, with a cabinet of 11 which contained only three other Nazis. Under these conditions, surely it would be easy enough to control him!

But the master of intrigue staged or took advantage of the burn-ing of the Reichstag, banned the communists, and conducted yet another election to the accompaniment of Nazi terror. This time the vote was 44% for the Nazis. With the assistance of the Catholic Centre Party, Hitler passed an Enabling Law which gave him dictatorial powers. When the President of the Republic (Hindenburg) died in 1934 Hitler united the offices of President and Chancellor, thus removing the Presidential veto and strengthening his position yet further. As a final step, he made himself head of the armed forces in 1938. In Taylor's words, "It had taken Hitler four years to destroy legality in Germany by legal means" (Taylor, 1975, p. 535).

Did Hitler ever get majority support? Did he need it? We can observe that in the last free elections support had declined to 33%, and that members of the Nazi Party comprised about 3% of the voting population. What was decisive was that the majority of the population were "drifters" who could not make up their minds whether they were for or against Hitler. Even at the end of the war, after defeat and the revelation of the atrocities of the camps, 60% were still drifters. This is what enabled the 10% fanatical Nazis (under skilled leadership) to get their way (Kettenacker, 1985). Many who were not fanatics had voted for Hitler, enticed by the many advantages offered by the Nazi Party. Michael Muller-Claudius, in skilful conversations with party members, estimated that 5% of Germans were fanatics who wished Jews to be exterminated. He conducted his probes by making such remarks as: "Well, so a start is being made at last in carrying out the programme against the Jews", and observed reactions. This kind of questioning is very sensitive to degrees of acquiescence, support and resistance. He found that the fanatics believed in the Jewish World Conspiracy. He also found that though the proportion of fanatics in his small sample remained unchanged from 1938 to 1942, the proportion of those who were concerned for the Jews declined. There was certainly widespread anti-semitism, but only a small proportion of the population was genocidal. An estimate — though very approximate — of the contribution of anti-semitism to Hitler's popularity can be made on the basis of Theodor Abel's (1938) study of 600 autobiographies of Nazi sympathizers, collected by offering cash prizes for "the best personal life history of an adherent of the Hitler movement". It is striking that 60% of the Hitler supporters in this sample make no mention of anti-semitism, concentrating on hunger in childhood, the loss of fathers during the war, and the pride and companionship of the Party. Of course, it is equally striking that 40% of them do make mention of anti-semitism! What is needed for the actions of a fanatical minority to succeed is the acquiescence and tacit support of the majority. Where there is no acquiescence, even the fanatics may be restrained.

We can see this in the resistance which developed to the Nazi euthanasia programme, designed to eliminate the mentally ill and mentally retarded. In spite of every disguise, the programme soon leaked to the general public and resistance to it was so widespread that it had to be abandoned. There was no such popular resistance to the extermination of the Jews. Why? After all, many Germans had been shocked by the destruction of Jewish property and businesses on Kristalnacht, in 1938; but much of the shock was prudential. It was felt that the behaviour of Nazi thugs had presented a picture of irresponsibility and vandalism to the world which would damage Germany's economic prospects and good standing. Why were they not similarly shocked by the extermination of the Jews? Part of the answer is that this was a programme carried out under wartime conditions and by then the opinion of the outside world did not matter. The other part of the answer must be that the Jews were not regarded as "part of us". In wartime, it is easier for governments to manipulate propaganda and censor or eliminate alternative sources of information. The way had been prepared. Jews had been stripped of their citizenship and their rights. They had been humiliated without redress. Methods of killing had been practised and perfected, to eliminate other unwanted subhumans.

In this account of genocide, I have stressed political leadership and strategic factors. We should not imagine that movements triumph automatically. Movements have to be led. Hitler was central to the creation and success of a genocidal party.

Justification

Hitler wrote in *Mein Kampf* that if the Jew triumphed, "this planet will sail empty of all life through the ether". What could he have meant? It seems that he should be read quite literally: Jews may look like human beings but they are not. They are subhuman. That is why everything possible had to be done to protect Aryans from Jewish contamination. The preservation of the Aryan race imposed a stern duty, namely the extermination of all contaminating races and groups: homosexuals, gypsies, Jews, the mentally ill. Racial hygiene was imperative in the cleansing of the *Volk*.

Evidence was amassed to show how Jews had displaced honest Germans in the professions of law, medicine, journalism and banking. Surely Germans were entitled to a place in their own country? Others who were at present hesitating to follow the German example would in the end applaud Germany's policies of racial and national hygiene. This is soberly explained in a publication entitled *Germany Speaks* by 21 leading members of party and state published in Great Britain in 1938. There is a strikingly posed photograph of the Fuhrer at the front and an appealing foreword by von Ribbentrop, extending the hand of friendship to all nations.

One of the learned chapters is by Dr Walter Gross, head of the Reich Bureau for Enlightenment on Population Policy and Racial Welfare. He links the control and prevention of hereditary diseases to the prevention of interracial marriages — particularly with Jews. The stages which lead to "the destruction of the vitality of a people and with it the destruction of the foundation of the state and culture as such are:

A decreasing population;
An increase in the hereditary unfit;
The promiscuous mingling of races."

All these conditions apply to Germany and urgent steps have to be taken to change them. Among the steps are sterilization of the unfit and the Nuremberg laws under which Jews are robbed of their Reich citizenship and become, in effect, stateless, and are prohibited from marrying Germans as well as from having "illicit" intercourse with them. Gross resorts to his equivalent of the bolshevik/capitalist pincer move of the Jews on German society: on the one hand, Jews contribute a higher percentage of crime than any other group since "the majority are from Eastern Europe" and on the other hand, they have imperialistic designs on German soil.

"During the political regimes of the past the Jews had managed to obtain an increasing hold on politics, art, culture and commerce. Since 1910, as many as 13 of them had immigrated every day into Germany from the East. " Thus Berlin had:

32.2 %	Jewish	chemists
47.9 %	"	doctors
50.2 %	"	lawyers
8.5 %	"	newspaper editors
14.2 %	"	producers and stage managers
37.5 %	"	dentists

"No people on earth with a vestige of pride in itself and its national honour will be willing to put up with such domination of the key professions by members of a completely alien race" (Gross, 1938, p. 76).

These are the measured tones of scientific propaganda for international consumption. They are far removed from the heated rhetoric of Hitler in his early days, but none the less deadly. Hitler supplied the whore and the intellectuals dressed it for the party. An example of his 1920 manner will illustrate.

Christian capitalism is already as good as destroyed, the international Jewish stock exchange capitalism gains in proportion as the other loses ground. . The one million workmen who were in Berlin in 1914 have remained what they were — they are workmen still, only thinner, worse clad, poor; but the 100,000 Jews from the East who entered Germany during the early days of the War — they arrived in poverty and they are now 'made men' riding in their motor cars: they have used the bodies of the people (*Volkskörper*) merely as a forcing ground for their own prosperity. The Jew has not grown poorer: he gradually gets bloated, and, if you don't believe me, I would ask you to go to one of our health resorts; there you will find two sorts of visitors: the German who goes there, perhaps for the first time in a long while, to breathe a little fresh air and to recover his health, and the Jew who goes there to lose his fat (Baynes, 1942, p.7).

This is a speech in the early years of Hitler's career, when there was little prospect of power. Yet the message did not change with the years. In a Reichstag speech of 1937 he says:

"For hundreds of years Germany was good enough to receive these elements [Jews], although they possessed nothing except infectious political and physical diseases."

As the Jew is demonized, the German becomes sacred. At first a victim, slow to realize how he has been exploited, he becomes an avenger, irresistible in wrath.

The Jews were vulnerable and poorly organized. There was little resistance from people who had, according to Nazi fantasy, organized an international conspiracy and super-state to destroy Germany.

The image of the Jew had been created in the preceding centuries. Hilberg (1985, vol 1) shows that almost every measure enacted by the Nazis had its precedent in Canonical law and pre-Nazi state development. Prohibition of intermarriage with Christians, exclusion from public office, marking of clothes, ghettoes, expropriation, pogroms and identification as Jews in official documents were among the many measures implemented. Hitler revived an image. He did not have to create one. It was as though he awakened Germans from a long sleep to confront a living nightmare. What they had always feared was actually happening. The Jews were taking over while their eyes had been closed.

Precipitation

There is no single event that precipitated the genocide. It took time to develop and it continued over a long time. It sprang from hatred and the desire to eliminate the Jews. Hilberg writes that what appears to be monolithic in fact consists of a "process of sequential steps that were taken at the initiative of countless decision makers in a far-flung bureaucratic machine" (Ibid. vol 1, p. 53). No one knew from the beginning how it would happen. There was a series of steps, each containing the "seed" of the next.

It appears that "the destruction process straddled two policies: emigration (1933-40) and annihilation (1941-45). In spite of this change of policies, the administrative continuity of the destruction process was unbroken" (Ibid. p. 54). The same steps that forced emigration could lead to annihilation. What were these steps? They were:

    *Defining Jews
    *Expropriating their property
    *Concentrating Jews into defined areas
    *Killing through deportation to extermination centres
and/ or by mobile killing squads *(einsatzgruppen)* in the occupied USSR.

If there is a precipitating event, it is the war, which seems to have signalled a change from forced emigration to annihilation. It is true that the destruction process must be understood as a whole, but it was responsive to events. The war stopped emigration. It also mobilized and empowered those who believed in extreme measures. Under the cloak of war many things could be done which would be difficult to do in peace time. People expect resolute steps against the enemy — secrecy, and killing. They can be fobbed off with reasons of state and emergency measures — should they make enquiries. The final solution was set in motion.

Annihilation

Mass killings started in 1940 and rose to a peak in 1942 under cover of war in the East. Polish Jews suffered most, with 3 million victims, and, after them, Russian Jews, with 700,000. The deaths, by year, were 100,000 in 1940; 1,100,000 in 1941; 2,700,000 in 1942; 500,000 in 1943; 600,000 in 1944 and 100,000 in 1945. The grand total is 5,100,000 (Hilberg, 1985, vol 3, p. 1220).

The details of this killing — the technology, the organization, the location of the camps, the barbaric experiments, the tortures, are beyond the scope of this book.

We can only recoil yet again at the spectacle of systematic murder by the state.

CHAPTER FOUR
POLITICIDE

"Thank you, the convalescence is going wonderfully well. I'm confident that the crushing of the Kazan Czechs and White Guards, as well as the kulak bloodsuckers who are supporting them, will be carried out with exemplary lack of mercy. With passionate greetings." (Lenin to Trotsky in Volkogonoff, 1991).

The UN definition of genocide which was quoted in Chapter 1 refers to an "intent to destroy, in whole or in part, a national, ethnical, racial or religious group, as such". It does not refer specifically to "political" groups, for the very good reason that many of the signatories were busy liquidating their own political opponents and were determined not to be hampered in their efforts. Yet in the contemporary world, political groups often occupy the place that religious groups had in former times, in that they are the repositories of the ideologies by which people live. They ought therefore to enjoy the same protection as religions. To persecute a political group is similar to persecuting a religious group. Whole "classes" have become the victims of modern political practice. What makes these "liquidations" genocidal is that the killing takes in the entire social base of a political opposition movement — men, women and children. They are, in the words of Chalk and Jonassohn (1990, p. 23), forms of "one-sided mass killing in which the state or other authority intends to destroy a group, as that group and membership in it are defined by the perpetrator". This is what makes the murder of the kulaks a proper subject for an account of genocide. They were a group defined and demonized by Lenin and Stalin and an attempt was made to liquidate them. Like witches, they were a fiction, but this does not mean that there were not procedures for identifying and destroying them. What it does mean is that the victims could not understand what they were being persecuted for, because their crime existed only in the imagination of their murderers. For practical purposes, kulaks were the peasantry, whether rich or poor. Similarly, the "bourgeoisie" of Cambodia was a wild fiction of the Khmer Rouge. For practical purposes, the bourgeoisie included any city dwellers and old regime loyalists. There is always this combination of feverish imagination and down-to-earth method in genocide, since very practical steps have to be taken to kill off large numbers of people, even if they are members of a non-existent category. (Or, to be more exact, they are marked down as belonging to a category whose members are identified by means of criteria which have nothing to do with the properties of the category.)

Those not privy to the fantasy of the perpetrators ask: "What have I done?" The proper answer is: "You are needed as a victim." But that is never the answer they are given and their confusion is never resolved.

The kulaks

> *"But I'm not guilty of anything!"*
> *"No one here is guilty of anything."*
> *"But why, then?"*
> *"Just because."*
>
> Tatyana Tolstoya

Who were the kulaks and why should they have become the victims of Lenin and Stalin? The shortest answer is that they were a bolshevik construct — demons of private ownership who deprived the workers of food. Kulaks were, mythologically, rich peasants who exploited the people and resisted collectivization. Class analysis was used to demonize them, but class analysis rapidly became a political convenience. The peasants, rich or poor, were seen as potential enemies of the state, and were thus marked for destruction. They possessed property, they resisted collectivization, their consciousness was pre-revolutionary, and they failed to deliver their quotas to the state. The use of the word "kulak" was extended to cover even very poor farmers, and the term "subkulak" was invented to reach those who might have thought themselves immune. In the same way, the term "sluggish schizophrenia" was later invented to reach political dissidents who might have been beyond the diagnosis of state psychiatrists. Words make the invisible visible to the eye of the skilled theorist.

It is possible that the murder of the kulaks and the establishment of slave labour camps were among the precedents for Hitler's concentration camps. He could hardly have been unaware of them. He also cited the concentration camps established by the British in the Anglo-Boer war of 1899-1902, but there was a qualitative leap from these to the horrors of slave labour, torture and extermination under Hitler and Stalin.

Preparation

The bolshevik government had gained power by trickery and violence. At the elections for the Constituent Assembly in November 1917, the social revolutionaries, whose power base included the peasants and the rural areas, got 410 of the 707 seats, whereas the bolsheviks got 175 seats — about a quarter. The only way to seize power was to abolish the Constituent Assembly and rely on force. It is interesting to observe that at no stage in its entire history did the Communist Party (unlike the Nazis) enjoy mass support — or anything like it. In June 1991, in the first fair test in seven decades, the communists attracted only 15% of the votes in the Russian Republic.

There was a history of conflict between the party and the peasants, right from the time of their failure to gain the peasant vote in the 1917 elections. This was attributed to peasant backwardness. Between 1918 and 1921, the bolsheviks fought a war against the peasants which overlapped with that civil war which, in the words of Robert Conquest, was merely "a contest between two well-armed but unpopular minorities"(1986, p.54). Collectivization was a dogma of the party; the peasants resisted. The peasant war resulted in 9 million deaths. It ended in a famine brought about by a crop requisition which removed from the peasants their means of subsistence. The results were predictable. Production declined. The state then declared that the kulaks "as a class" had to be liquidated. This decision led to something like 14,500,000 additional deaths.

Justification

The justification was Marxist-Leninist theory according to which private property had to be abolished in order to achieve the dictatorship of the proletariat. Only when all property was owned by the state — acting as an agent of the people — would the socialist revolution be complete. The kulaks clung to private property and were an obstacle to the achievement of the classless society. Since they continued to represent the perspective and interests of private property, they were enemies of the people. They were obstacles to progress and had proved this by not voting for the bolsheviks in 1917 and by failing to meet their crop quotas.

Precipitation

Stalin was consolidating his power in a bitter internal struggle, and one of his principal weapons was ideological. Industrialization and collectivization were to proceed according to pure Marxist principles. Besides, the peasants were still not meeting their quotas. If they were allowed to get away with it, who might not try next? Under the New Economic Policy they had been allowed to grow "rich", yet they had not delivered. The problem appeared to be the "goods famine" in the country. The peasants could get none of the things they needed in return for their grain. They needed machinery and useful industrial products. Instead, they got paper money which could buy nothing. Again it looked as though they were being swindled. The result is that by 1927 a grain crisis was looming — and with it a political crisis.

Two responses were discussed. The first was to attempt to increase grain production and to extract grain from the peasants by legal means and economic measures. In other words, one should make it worth their while to produce and to sell. After all, extreme coercion had been used for a decade and had failed to improve the situation. The other response was to step up the use of force. Stalin threw his opponents off balance by apparently approving the moderate approach while issuing orders for the use of force. In this way he captured the support and enthusiasm of the militant left-wing tendency, still undaunted in their pursuit of utopia by extreme measures. Surely, after so much suffering, only a little more was required to attain the millennium. How could they falter when they were so close? Stalin ordered drastic measures so that they would not be cheated of socialism by the greed of the last capitalists in their midst — the kulaks. The great terror had begun. The militants would discover what terror could do; the whole of Soviet society would discover the meaning of terror. Yet the problems of food supply were not solved because the means employed were fundamentally incompatible with the ends being sought. One cannot achieve agricultural production by destroying the most enterprising producers and terrifying the rest into sullen conformity, as Stalin hoped.

In a speech to a conference of Marxist agrarians Stalin explained: "From a policy of limiting the exploitative tendencies of the kulaks, we have gone over to a policy of liquidating the kulaks as a class."

Liquidation

How does one liquidate a class? The first thing to do is to convert the word by which they are described into a term of hatred and contempt. This was what happened. The term "kulak" came to mean all that was contemptibly selfish and profiteering in the midst of hunger and shortages. The kulaks were enemies of the state, the people, the revolution. They were caricatured and derided. They were presented to the people as the cause of their suffering. This was why the revolution was not working. The word "dekulakization" entered the vocabulary of politics to describe the crusade against the kulaks. Hundreds of thousands of families had their farms confiscated and were transported to remote areas. According to Volkogonov (1991) 150,000 families were exiled to Siberia and the North in 1929, 240,000 in 1930, and 285,000 in 1931.The process continued. And we should note that these are families, not individuals. Millions died of hunger and disease; others were shot. How many? Conquest estimates 14,500,000; Volkogonov is unable to reach a final estimate.

Collectivization went ahead, but production went down. The result could only be disaster, especially since food quotas were extracted without regard to local need. A vast area stricken by famine was created in the Ukraine, the Volga, the northern Caucasus and other regions. Prominent American journalists such as Duranty of *The New York Times* and Fischer of *The Nation* played a disgraceful role in this by concealing the famine and the killing that was going on. At first they did not report the famine and later, when it had been reported by Malcolm Muggeridge in the *Manchester Guardian*, they denied it (Mace 1988).

Russian agriculture was retarded for decades, but Stalin had increased his personal power. His liquidation of the kulaks had demonstrated the use of terror. He had perfected the means. Now no one could resist him.

He turned on his enemies and the first were those who had been his "best friends" and at the forefront of the revolution. In this, the Russian Revolution repeated the pattern of the French, which had purged itself of 85% of its leaders in farcical trials culminating in the guillotine. The Russian revolutionaries had feared that this might happen; Bukharin had gone so far as to draft an "anti-Thermidorian Catechism" of rules to prevent fratricidal quarrels; but it was in vain (Deutscher and Deutscher, 1984). Stalin was a more thorough and hideous Robespierre. The technique was the same. Revolutionaries were accused of being agents of foreign powers. The more ardently they had worked for the revolution, the more diabolical the disguise. The greater the apparent loyalty to the cause, the deeper the betrayal. There could be no successful defence against this paradoxical reasoning. It had worked in the aftermath of the French Revolution and it worked again. Revolutionaries were condemned by their own apparent zeal. Behind every appearance there was a terrifying reality.

Those who use terror must fear terror. In the pursuit of their ideals, the revolutionaries had divided the world into absolute good and absolute bad. They fought the bad without scruple, but it multiplied on every side. It seemed that the liquidation of class enemies could never stop.

Khmer Rouge politicide in Kampuchea

Question: *"Why did your revolution fail?"*

Pol Pot: *"Because we totally underestimated the number of Vietnamese spies in our society. Even if we had got down to a million Khmers [out of 6/7 million], provided they were patriots, we could have built a great and glorious Kampuchea."* [Kampuchea was what Cambodia came to be called under the Khmer Rouge.]

Jean-Baptiste Carrier: *"We shall turn France into a cemetery rather than fail in her regeneration."* [At the time of the French Revolution.]

Introduction

The victims of the Cambodian revolution can be described, rather loosely, as the bourgeoisie. They were, on the whole, urban dwellers, educated people, professionals, and property owners. They had been contaminated by westernization. They were said to have been corrupted by American aid and they were the spiritual descendants of those who had collaborated with colonizers. But at the same time, ethnic enemies such as the Muslim Cham and Vietnamese were murdered. To understand the Khmer Rouge terror and the extermination of city dwellers in even the most rudimentary way it is necessary to make a quick sketch of the situation as it was in Cambodia in the 1970s.

When Phnom Penh fell to the Khmer Rouge in 1975, it was almost a relief, even to those who had most to fear. Once again a corrupt client of an intrusive superpower had been overthrown. Once again it had been shown that superior weapons cannot subdue superior morale. Those who believe in the cause can defeat those who believe in their comfort. But what sort of cause was this?

As soon as they had occupied Phnom Penh, the Khmer Rouge began a forced evacuation of its 3 million inhabitants. The terror of the process can be seen in its beginnings: a platoon of young Khmer Rouge soldiers marched to the hospital and ordered those who could walk to get out of their beds and push those who could not in a forced march out of the city. "From hospitals all over the city crawled and hobbled the casualties of war. . . . Men with no legs bumped down stairs . . . blind boys laid their hands on the shoulders of crippled guides, soldiers with one foot and no crutches . . . parents carried their wounded children in plastic bags that oozed blood . . . (Shawcross, 1986, p. 366). This is a scene from hell — or war in the twentieth century. The killing continued from 1975 to 1979 when the Khmer Rouge were defeated by the Vietnamese. How many were killed by the regime of Democratic Kampuchea (as it came to be known)? Perhaps "at most" a million (Burgler, 1990), perhaps 2 million (Ponchaud, 1978). It is difficult to be accurate. Between 1 and 2 million is as close as we can get in these times of mass murder.

The story continues. In spite of its reputation for mass murder, the regime of Democratic Kampuchea became the officially accredited government at the UN in 1981 (gaining 77 votes to 37, with 31 abstentions). No matter how monstrous a regime is, it can take its place at the United Nations. (The Vietnamese, as an invading force, were called upon in 1979 to withdraw from Cambodia by 91 votes to 21, with 21 abstentions, in spite of the fact that they brought the Cambodian genocide to an end.) No UN action was taken to halt the killing in Kampuchea, since the powerplay of China, the Soviet Union and the USA, each with its own clients in the region, paralyzed the world body. The Soviet Union supported the Vietnamese-backed People's Revolutionary Council, whereas US policy was dictated by opposition to Vietnam. China opposed the Vietnamese takeover even to the extent of attempting armed intervention — a move which failed within 6 weeks. Thailand supported the Khmer Rouge because it feared the Vietnamese presence on its borders. One of the most extraordinary of the extraordinary ironies of the war is that

UNICEF and the International Red Cross were forced to feed the Khmer Rouge before they were allowed to feed the children of Kampuchea. After the Vietnamese invasion of Kampuchea, the Thais and Chinese began supplying the Khmer Rouge. To relieve the burden on themselves, they insisted that part of the international aid destined for Kampuchea be diverted to the Khmer Rouge.

After this introductory sketch, let us look more systematically at the events leading up to genocide.

Preparation

The seeds of the genocidal conflict lay in the processes of colonization and decolonization, in that some of the divisions created in the colonial period were of importance later on and in the sense that the wars of decolonization in South East Asia led to the genocide.

Cambodia had been a French Protectorate since 1863 and resistance to French rule had commenced almost immediately. A French practice which poisoned relations with the Khmers (Cambodians) was to staff its administration with Vietnamese. A communist presence was established in the 1930s, when the Indochina Communist Party was formed in 1930, in Hong Kong, under the leadership of Ho Chi Minh. When France fell to Germany in 1940, a freedom movement (Khmer Issarak) was established. In the war, the Japanese disappointed Cambodian activists, who had naturally hoped for Japanese support for Asian independence from European imperialists, by recognizing the Vichy government of France and accordingly recognizing its jurisdiction in Cambodia. The Japanese strategy was to form pacts with Thailand and Vichy France while it attended to more pressing matters in its war against Great Britain and the USA. It was only in March 1945 that the Japanese removed the French administration and replaced it with a Cambodian government. This was too late for the Cambodians to strengthen their position. By August the Japanese had surrendered and two months later French rule had been reimposed (Chandler, 1983). But this taste had strengthened the desire for independence. Communism seemed to offer the best recipe for the struggle, as in so many parts of the colonized world. There was the possibility of Soviet assistance, diplomatic if not military; and there was the heady appeal of a doctrine which would enable the intellectuals to rule on behalf of the people. It was a pure vision in a corrupt world.

By 1949 the French had granted a qualified independence; by 1953 independence was complete. And by 1954 the French had been defeated at Dien Bien Phu in neighbouring Vietnam. This might have been the end of the story had it not been for the cold war and superpower rivalry. According to the "domino" theory, if Vietnam fell to communists, the rest of South East Asia might follow. The degree of foreign involvement in the affairs of the region can be seen from the fact that the Geneva Agreements of 1954 which recognized Cambodian neutrality were signed by France, the Soviet Union, the People's Republic of China and North Vietnam. The attachment of the signatures of the Soviet Union and of China automatically meant the absence of the signature of the USA, which did not recognize Cambodian neutrality. By refusing to join the South East Asia Treaty Organization (SEATO), an anti-communist organization dominated by the USA, Cambodia became suspect; and Thailand and South Vietnam were encouraged to harass the Cambodian army. Even more directly, the CIA gave support to a guerilla force called the Khmer Serei (Free Khmer). In spite of this, the Cambodians attempted to remain neutral in the superpower struggle, a hopeless quest in a situation of this kind, where to be neutral is to be of the enemy party. The only question, in the words of an Irish joke, is whether you are a neutral communist or a neutral capitalist. Cambodia renounced all US aid in 1963 and severed diplomatic relations in 1965, proving beyond all doubt to the US that it was a communist neutral. Anyway, there was no room for that kind of neutrality in the cold war.

Prince Sihanouk, the Cambodian Prime Minister, was faced with two problems which he could not resolve: aid had brought corruption and the North Vietnamese continued to use Cambodian territory as a supply route and a base in their war against South Vietnam and, of course, the USA. If he got rid of aid, all sorts of complaints could be expected from those who had benefited: the military budget would have to be cut; civil servants would no longer receive the bribes to which they had become accustomed; the commercial classes would feel the pinch; and students would no longer be able to find the jobs they felt entitled to. Yet if he continued accepting aid, he could not be neutral. He could not stop the North Vietnamese from using Cambodian territory without becoming deeply involved in the Vietnam War. The problem was solved for him by a coup. The Cambodian army (the most substantial losers when American aid was rejected) and the CIA removed him from office and installed Lon Nol. In this way, Sihanouk was thrown into the arms of the Khmer Rouge, backed by China and North Vietnam.

Lon Nol, in his years of misrule, demonstrated the truth that governments are not overthrown, they destroy themselves. He was a dependent of the USA, which then proceeded to treat him with the contempt reserved for dependents. A joint US and South Vietnam invasion of Cambodia was launched to clear out the North Vietnamese, but without informing Lon Nol until it was under way. His approval was taken for granted. This was the beginning of the end. Lon Nol could only be kept in power by US support; but the US government was under domestic pressure to withdraw from Vietnam and to abandon all its commitments. Few things are less reliable than the friendships of Great Powers — as the Armenians found when all the European powers, though friendly, were not friendly enough to act against the Turks. Meanwhile the combination of huge financial aid, an unreliable military government, and lack of common purpose had their predictable effect within Cambodia. Those who had the opportunity to enrich themselves did so. Officers created phantom soldiers and units in order to draw their pay, while real soldiers who were actually fighting sometimes waited for months to be paid. The country was rich only in bribes and rackets. Having a good time was the most important thing.

In the meanwhile, the Khmer Rouge were advancing. Where had they come from?

We have already seen that the Indochina Communist Party (ICP) was formed in 1930. During the Second World War, armed Khmer groups were formed, and some of their leaders were members of the ICP. Though these movements grew in the immediate postwar period, they did not have a smooth rise to success. After the Geneva Agreements in 1954 the insurgents were weakened by pressure from both the Soviet Union and China to lay down arms. Some communist insurgents went to Hanoi, some abandoned armed activity, and a few went into hiding and continued the work of the Khmer People's Revolutionary Party. But for events which weakened the government, they would probably have remained unimportant.

Since several of the leaders are still potentially powerful, it is worth saying something about their education and ideas. They were a group who had studied in France where they had absorbed their revolutionary ideas — not so much from the French as from other foreign students. In 1949 Pol Pot (Saloth Sar) had received a scholarship to study at the École Française de Radioeléctricité. He failed his examinations three times running, perhaps partly because he devoted much of his time to a Marxist circle of Cambodian students in Paris, probably affiliated to the French Communist Party. At the same time, Chinese, Vietnamese and other Marxist groups were thriving in Paris. It was there that he and Ieng Sary, who was also to be important as a revolutionary, became related by marriage, since their wives were sisters. This was the beginning of the pattern of relationships which characterized the ruling group in Phnom Penh 20 years later. "By 1978 the government appears to have been in the hands of about ten people related not only by intellectual training and shared revolutionary experience but also by marriage" (Shawcross, 1986, p. 381). While still a student, Pol Pot visited Yugoslavia and admired the massive labour mobilization on capital works projects and the enforced collectivization of farming which he saw. By the time Belgrade had reverted to a policy of fostering private peasant agriculture, he was back in Paris (Kiernan, 1985). At the same time Ieng Sary was studying Stalin's writings and was apparently impressed by his methods of control.

After his return to Cambodia, Pol Pot worked as a teacher and journalist. He joined a communist party cell and was set to working with the masses under Vietnamese supervision. He resented this because he was not acknowleged as an intellectual.

Khieu Samphan, another significant figure in the Khmer Rouge, completed a thesis on *Cambodia's Economy and Industrial Development* at the University of Paris in 1959. He argued that integration into the world economy would retard Cambodia's development, that the cities were parasites on the countryside where 90% of the people lived, and that workers should be transferred from cities into productive work in the countryside. Only after agriculture had been developed and modernized could an independent industry take off, since foreign investment merely led to the penetration of foreign goods. Likewise, foreign aid merely increased the import of luxury goods and created a wasteful commercial and service class in the cities, most of whom were engaged in unproductive work as waiters, maids, cycle drivers, civil servants, and restaurateurs. Wealth is the equivalent of corruption, it seems. His belief that industrial development and modernization could be reversed by persuasion rather than by force are not indications of moderation but of adolescent idealism and immaturity. Under other circumstances, he might well have realized their fatuity. You cannot take away people's ways of earning their living, move urban workers to the countryside to labour on projects of which they know nothing and in places which do not concern them, and halt production by isolating an economic system from the rest of the world without extreme violence — unless you are doing it on paper and in a thesis.

These were exactly the sort of leaders who could produce the most mischief. They were shallow intellectuals, school teachers, economists without experience, journalists, idealists. They also became skilled revolutionaries and practitioners of violence.

Justification

In the ideology of the Khmer Rouge, the struggle was between "the people" and "the underpeople". The people were the workers, peasants and members of the Khmer Rouge, whereas the underpeople were the commercial and service classes, as well as professionals and those contaminated by middle class values. Very roughly, they were the bourgeoisie. Civil servants, doctors, lawyers, soldiers of the Cambodian government, teachers, commercial people of all sorts, and other unproductive parasites were the target. They were impurities in the body of the nation. "What is rotten must be removed." "What is infected must be cut out." And, even more ominously, "Their line must be annihilated down to the last survivor." These were the slogans that were endlessly repeated (Ponchaud, 1978).

At the beginning of this account of the Cambodian genocide I have cited Pol Pot. We see that he is similar to all ideological perpetrators of genocide. He believes in purity. He believes that it can be achieved by killing, and that the killing should continue until the purification has been achieved, even if it means reducing a nation of 7 million to 1 million.

The roots of the proposed transformation of society were the shallow economic ideas outlined above, grafted onto Marxist theory and Stalinist methods. These ideas would have remained insignificant had they not arisen in a country being devastated by both American aid and American bombing. The bombing showed that the government was unable to protect its sovereignty. The military aid converted Cambodia into a client state. Violence and corruption were the deadly machines which destroyed all that was stable in Cambodian society.

After the revolution, history was to begin again, at least in Kampuchea (Cambodia). At the the fall of Phnom Penh, on April 17, 1975, the calendar was turned back to the Year Zero (we are reminded of the French Revolution and its ambition to start the history of mankind afresh). All were to live under the guidance of the *Angka* (Supreme Organization), the philosophy of which could be summed up as the rejection of individualism, the surrender of will to the collective, the rejection of all that was corrupt and foreign (even drugs, medicine and economic aid), and a reversion to the agricultural past so thorough that it meant the destruction of every form of 'bourgeois' life. The creation of a New Man was the object, and to achieve this the past had to be annihilated by the future and the old made to obey the young. People had to learn to renounce everything personal — attitudes, material goods, family. As is usual in such revolutionary organizations, the cadres of the *Angka* first destroyed their external enemies and then turned on their own. The new victims were accused of being agents of Vietnam.

Precipitation

Four events precipitated the takeover of Cambodia by the Khmer Rouge. The first was the replacement of Sihanouk by Lon Nol, with CIA assistance. Sihanouk had attempted to preserve Cambodian neutrality and for this reason he was unpopular with the US. However, once he had been removed from the government, he joined forces with the Khmer Rouge and they used his popularity with the peasants for their own purposes. Lon Nol was quite easily identified as a puppet who served foreign interests.

The second was the combined US and South Vietnamese invasion of Cambodia in 1970 without advance notice to Lon Nol. The purpose of the invasion was to destroy North Vietnamese bases and to deny the North Vietnamese the use of supply routes running through Cambodia; the effect was to antagonize the Cambodian peasants and to expose Lon Nol's position as an American stooge. If he did not know in advance of the invasion, then he was too insignificant to be consulted by his masters; if he did know, then he was responsible for the invasion of his own country by foreign powers. The Americans withdrew within two months, but the South Vietnamese stayed for a year, antagonizing the local population by rape, theft and murder. North Vietnamese troops were not eliminated; instead, they were driven deeper into the centre of Cambodia where they shielded the Khmer Rouge from Cambodian government troops, enabling them to rally and organize for a showdown. In early 1970 the Khmer Rouge had a strength of 800 men under arms; a little over a year later, they had 35,000. With this force, and assisted by the North Vietnamese, they decisively defeated the Cambodian government forces backed by the US, at Chenla.

The third event was the killing of four students and the wounding of eleven more in May 1970 by the National Guard at Kent State University in Ohio. The invasion of Cambodia had revived the anti-war demonstrations; the killing of students was the turning point for Nixon. After the invasion, a third of American colleges and universities were closed by demonstrations; after the deaths at Kent State, about 100,000 protesters converged on Washington, surrounded the White House with buses, and threatened invasion. Or, at least, invasion is what Alexander Haig feared. Troops had been brought into the White House to repel an attack. The White House was at war with an articulate and intelligent section of the youth of America and their anxious elders, disturbed by pointless and profitless interference in distant countries. After this, the pressure on the White House to withdraw from Vietnam and to cease from intervention in neighbouring states became relentless.

The final precipitating event was the secret American bombing of Cambodia in 1973, again in a fruitless attempt to eliminate North Vietnamese bases. In eight months US bombers dropped more than 3 times the amount of bombs they had released over Japan in World War II — 539,129 tons. This did not have the intended effect of eliminating the North Vietnamese; instead they were driven deeper into Cambodia. It did have the entirely predictable effect of proving to Cambodians that the US was waging an imperialist, capitalist, colonialist, racist war against a helpless people who had never done them any harm. The flame was lit. What could be more holy than a crusade to kill those who had collaborated with such an enemy — especially one masquerading as a friend?

The genocide

The leaders, trained in Paris to separate theory from reality by the greatest possible distance, wished to establish the most advanced form of communism in the world. The educational process which they had commenced abroad was continued in revolutionary activity against "the Sodoms" of the cities into which American aid was pouring. The shame of seeing one's country reduced to a puppet left a stain which only radical cleansing could remove. Purity and the revival of ancient glory were what the revolutionaries sought. The youthful army was drilled in revolutionary slogans by the cadres. They learnt to choose between the purity of the Angka and the shame of living under a puppet regime. Defeated commanders were liquidated. The revolution could have no mercy if it was to succeed. "What is rotten must be removed." Soldiers trained in pitiless battle were drilled by cadres who served a pitiliess theory. Society had to be purified. This could only be done by emptying the corrupt cities and returning to the past. Parents had to be taught to honour and obey their children since only the young had not yet been corrupted. The children were to learn their science from the workers and peasants who had also not been corrupted. All who had been corrupted — by education, class or employment (except the "intellectuals" of the movement) had to be liquidated. The drive to eliminate all impurities and isolate the country from further contamination included the refusal of foreign aid. Food and medicines were rejected. The corrupt died or were killed. Hundreds of thousands died under the frightful conditions of forced labour on a starvation diet. Purification encompassed the liquidation of ethnic groups: Buddhists, Cham Muslims and Chinese were virtually eliminated in programmes of "ethnic cleansing". This continued until the Vietnamese invaded Cambodia on 25 December 1978. Unexpectedly, since they had planned for a two-year war, they met with little resistance and reached Phnom Penh in three weeks. Cambodians who had been reduced to despair welcomed them as saviours.

The international response to this invasion was dictated by Cold War allegiances. Australia, Denmark, England, Japan and Sweden, among others, reduced or cancelled their aid programmes to Vietnam. The Pol Pot regime was supported on the grounds that the internal affairs of a country are its own business. China attacked Vietnam and was humiliated within four weeks, but only after causing immense damage.

What lay behind this adoption of a high moral stance? Certainly not indignation about the genocide. Vietnam was a client of the Soviet Union; China was determined to become the regional superpower with Kampuchea (Cambodia) as its client; the powers which had cancelled their aid to Vietnam were more nervous about any extension of Soviet influence than they were about an extension of American influence. The fact that the US had bungled its affairs in South East Asia made Soviet influence all the more threatening. In the difficult manoeuvres of international diplomacy the weak often perish to the accompaniment of high sentiment. The Vietnamese had ended the genocide in Cambodia, but for this they received no thanks.

CHAPTER FIVE

EXPLAINING GENOCIDE

"The decisive part in the subjugation of the intelligentsia was played not by terror and bribery. . . but by the word 'Revolution', which none of them could bear to give up." (Nadezhda Mandelstam)

A J.P. Taylor once remarked that the French Revolution was the first modern revolution: it was to inaugurate the first state ever to be founded on Reason. There had been theocracies founded on faith; there had even been democracies providing degrees of equality; but there had never before been a state which was to be constructed like a theorem in political geometry. Given the axioms of liberty, equality and fraternity, the design of the state would follow — QED. There had been killing before, for political purposes, but never had there been such rational killing. In the past, there had been coups and insurrections; or one sect had displaced another; but no one had ever served universal reason. Faith, yes. God, yes. But who would ever have thought it worth following Reason? Reason was the new God. Ever since the old God, full of grumbles and whims and paradoxes, had been replaced by an algorithm and the universe had become a species of clock, it had become essential for those in harmony with the times to discover the algorithm and unlock the secrets of the universe. Suddenly, intellectuals were important. They devised constitutions; who else was fit to do so? They studied physics and chemistry and dreamt of a science of history (in this book we show signs of this disease). All this culminated in the two greatest intellectual groundplans of our time: the Hegelian and then the Marxist theories of history. The world is an idea. God is thought, thinking itself. Does it matter much if we reverse Hegel and make ideas dependent upon the material world? Whether it is the World as Idea, or the Idea of the World that is important, the intellectuals retain their place. Theirs is the task of understanding the relentless machinery thumping away in the boiler-room of history, from thesis to antithesis to synthesis like one of these new-fangled steam pumps. No one must get in the way of the machine. If you do, too bad for you! In this way, the intellectuals become the engineers of history, fussing over its design. But since history is really History, and reason is really Reason — (God has changed shape but is the same implacable old cannibal) — the fuss takes the old sacrificial forms. Except that sacrifice and superstition are now modern and more thorough than ever. The modern ideologues are the old theologues. All that has happened is that an ideocracy has replaced a theocracy. There is the same lust to conclude every syllogism with an execution (which is, after all, the only really sincere conclusion).

The French Revolution was certainly modern. It overthrew scepticism. It made tolerance and laxity into intellectual errors — bugs introduced surreptitiously into the algorithm of history. Such fury against sinning was not new, but the new rationalists experienced themselves as New Men, the first ever in an Age Without Superstition. They were the servants/masters of the world as machine/idea. The universe is a machine, society is a machine, the state is a machine, people are body-machines. This is the totalitarian idea of modernism. Political modernists tend the machine; postmodernists collect the garbage. And make a collage of it.

These few remarks may guide us as we examine genocide scenarios. How should they be classified? Is there only one scenario, or are there many, and are they all different? It may be that genocides can be divided into two main categories: ideological and pragmatic. Some such distinction may serve us well. Ideological genocides are those which attempt to impose a vision on the world. They change meaning. Not content with changing the composition of society, the ideological genocide decides to change its significance. Ideological genocides may proceed by faith (in the old manner) or by reason (in the modern).

In this sense, the bolsheviks are modern ideologues and the

fascists, nationalists and Nazis are pre-modern. Bolshevism is a serious intellectual enterprise, with serious intellectuals trying to devise serious machine-states which run from here straight into the future. Nazism, nationalism and fascism are reactions to modernity. They try to restore blood and guts to politics. Their demonology and anthropology go back to ancient times. The Hobbits would know where they were in a Nazi state. It is difficult to realise that the cliche of the nation-state belongs to this set of catastrophic theories. Usually it lies dormant in the politician's catechism as one of those articles of faith that no one bothers to understand. In this condition, it is as harmless as belief in the resurrection; yet from time to time someone sets out to purify the nation, and then we see just how crazy and dangerous the idea is, because the almost inevitable consequences of trying to achieve the nation-state are large scale operations of purification and "ethnic cleansing". How do these operations work? We can either move populations from A to B and from B to A in order to achieve greater homogeneity, or we can liquidate those in the wrong place.

Pragmatic genocides are genocides devoid of vision. The important thing in classifying genocides is to recognize the primary goal of the killing. If the primary goal is to show who's boss and to eliminate other possible bosses, the genocide is pragmatic. Such genocides are driven by fear, by a desire for revenge, or by a wish to make examples so that enemies will not give further trouble. A pyramid of skulls is a useful deterrent.

Events and objects cannot be divided into categories which are absolutely different from each other. All that we can claim for our two categories is that the events within them differ in certain interesting respects. If we have a dimension with two poles at opposite ends — one ideological, one practical — then events which cluster at one end differ from events which cluster at the other in the degree to which they are theory-driven as opposed to practical. This does not mean that there is no practice at the theory end of the continuum or no theory at the practical end. It simply means that we focus on the degree of difference.

What we should do now is look at a number of cases to see whether these generalizations hold. If we consider the cases we have descibed, the following division seems natural:

Ideological
Nazi genocide of Jews and gypsies
Stalinist genocide of kulaks
Khmer Rouge genocide of "bourgeoisie"
Turkish genocide of Armenians

Pragmatic
German genocide of Herero
Postcolonial genocide of Ibo

The main test of ideological genocides is that they attempt to transform the meaning of society by imposing one theory or faith on everyone and killing those who cannot, or are judged unfit to accept it. By contrast, pragmatic genocides are not interested in the views which people may hold or in their anthropological "essence". If people are not a threat or if they can't be robbed, they are usually left alone once the frenzy is over.

We must now ask two further questions. The first is whether this classification holds when a larger set of cases is examined. The second is whether it can be refined to give a more detailed picture of genocides. The more detailed, the more useful the scenarios are likely to be. There have been several attempts to classify genocides. Here I shall draw on those of Fein, Kuper, and Harff and Gurr. Harff and Gurr (1988) also provide us with an extended set of genocides, identifying 40 between the end of World War II and 1988. We can construct a table on the basis of the work done by these scholars.

TYPOLOGY OF GENOCIDES/POLITICIDES

Fein	*Kuper*	*Harff and Gurr*
developmental	against indigenes	hegemonic
despotic	decolonization	repressive
retributive	retributive	retributive
ideological	ideological	revolutionary
		xenophobic

The correspondence of the terms is not exact but there is enough agreement for us to be able to extract some terms without difficulty.

The first thing to observe is that it is not difficult to recognize the split between ideological and pragmatic genocides. All the authors identify an ideological form of genocide. Harff and Gurr (1988, p. 363) write that revolutionary genocide is "mass murder of class or political enemies in the service of new revolutionary ideologies". To this we can add the concept of ideological xenophobia as in the Nazi and the Armenian cases, where the purpose was to purify the nation by eliminating all alien elements. We then end up with two forms of ideological genocide which can be defined as genocide of the Left and of the Right — i.e. of modernism and anti-modernism to the genocides of modernism and anti-modernism. Both are ideological: they differ through being driven by different theories.

Revolutionary genocide in our time is often in the service of progressive ideals, its impulse rational and universal. It is Marxist and modern and appeals to the intelligentsia in general and academics engaged in the social sciences in particular. It often takes the specific form of politicide — or the killing of members of political groupings, movements and parties rather than of ethnic groups or nationalities. Thus, the killing of the kulaks in the Soviet Union was politicide — the extermination of a faction or class construed as deliberately opposing the policy of collectivization. No matter if the kulaks did not construe themselves as a political movement. No matter that no sober historical assessment could conceivably have construed them as a political movement in any way. They were so construed by Lenin and Stalin and relentlessly persecuted as an obstacle, a political anachronism and a counter-revolutionary force. It is the perpetrators of genocide (or politicide) who do the defining. This is the prerogative of power.

What of pragmatic genocides, driven by fear, hatred, material needs and the desire to dominate? Theory is rudimentary, though some mimicry may occur. Noticeably absent though is the influence of intellectuals. Ideas, such as they are, come off the peg. There are no theorists writing books or treatises for discussion in seminars or lecture halls. Applying Levi-Strauss' distinctions, discourse is raw rather than cooked. Where the ideologues write massive romances about the destiny of the people, the nature of the enemy and the course of history (even Hegel's philosophy has been called a *Bildungsroman* — one of those great formative epics — by George Steiner), the pragmatists reduce things to the self-evident. There are enemies. They are dangerous. Half measures are not enough because the survivors will take revenge. Better to do things thoroughly. To make an example of them will have a salutary effect on any others who may be thinking of rebelling. The ideologues reconstruct reality, the pragmatists accept it. For the ideologue, the main question is: What kind of story could be told about the world which would make it worthy of my presence? For the pragmatist, the main question is: How do I get by in the kind of story the world is.

Now, back to the cupboard and let's see what's left on the shelves. One item that stands out immediately is retributive genocide. It is listed by all the authors. A retributive genocide is very much a practical affair. Someone has injured you in the past. It is therefore only sensible to do them in before they have a second chance. This often occurs in the wake of decolonization or at the end of a war, because some distinct group has been used by the colonizers or the invaders against the rest of the population. (Invaders and colonizers have been using this device for centuries.) The trick is to find a minority group with good reason not to like the majority of the people. Then use them to govern the rest. They will become extremely unpopular and totally dependent on you. In the Ottoman Empire, Christian eunuchs were used at one time. They had no descendents, they did not form rival dynasties, and they were unable to make revolutionary appeals to the local population. They were wholly committed to the Sultan. Today, the castration of public servants is no longer regarded as politically viable but the general formula remains a good one. Hence the Harkis in Algeria, the Hutu in Burundi and the Tamil in Sri Lanka were singled out for advancement by their colonial masters and subsequent massacre by the revolutionary movements. The lesson is: when bestowing political loyalties, pay no attention to the promises of the powers you pledge yourself to serve. Ask yourself simply: What is it in their selfish interests to do? That is what they will do. The departing powers will promise to look after their collaborators until the very last moment since that is the only way to keep them loyal. Then they will abandon them.

The next form of genocide which stands out is what Fein calls developmental genocide and Kuper calls genocide against indigenous peoples. Harff and Gurr subsume developmental genocides under hegemonial genocides. What are developmental genocides? The usual pattern is for colonizers to arrive to occupy a land and exploit it. The people they encounter are technologically unsophisticated and have a different economy and way of life. The colonized are organized in tribal systems and are politically weaker than the invaders, who have a well-developed sense of their own superiority. They have a superior religion, a superior culture, a superior economy and superior brains. They often believe that development and progress make the displacement of the indigenous people essential. The process is driven by a million small contacts in which the invaders extract rewards from the natives, or profit by displacing them. It is justified by new assumptions and rules of property. What belongs to everyone belongs to no one and may therefore be used and owned by the invaders. Those who can use the land more efficiently should own the land. We have seen how this happened in German South West Africa. It is happening to the present day in Brazil. Consider the conflict between Bushmen hunter-gatherers and Tswana cattle-herders in Botswana (which is simply the last act of a conflict between two ways of life which has been going on for the last two centuries in southern Africa). The hunter-gatherers need large tracts of land unoccupied by humans to continue their way of life. They are organized into small groups with only the most rudimentary political structure and resources. The pastoralists are part of the dominant society. They require land for their cattle. They are better organized than the Bushmen. Botswana society is their society — at least in any systematic conflict with the Bushmen. If there has to be a choice between two ways of life then there is no doubt which way the state will choose. The herding of cattle is rational; the old ways of hunting are not. The land can be exploited more efficiently by herders. The result is that Bushmen have been resettled in camps. Those who live in the Central Kalahari Game Reserve are also being subjected to pressure to move into camps.

Gradually, their land has been taken away from them. This has been going on since 1847, when white settlers arrived in Ghanzi and claimed tracts of land; it continued with the granting of farms of up to 10,000 hectares to Tswana ranchers by the Botswana government in 1980. It is estimated that of the 39,000 Bushmen in Botswana only 3,000 still live the hunter-gatherer life of their ancestors. It appears that Bushmen hunting on ancestral lands that are now fenced off as private and state property have been subjected to torture by Officers of the Department of Wildlife and National Parks (Kelso, 1992).

What is to be done? Mineral prospectors and ranchers are contending for the lands of the Bushmen. Land which is earmarked for them is coveted by those with wealth and influence. In 1991 three farms set aside for Bushman development were being diverted to officials until the Norwegian government used the threat of suspending aid to compel the Botswana government to intervene. We cannot expect the pressure on the Bushmen to diminish in a competitive world. Each culture must be able to protect itself, though it may be fortunate enough to receive help from time to time. Permanent dependency means eventual dispossession. The Bushmen grasp this truth. They want the government to grant them part of the land of their ancestors and to pay compensation for the rest. But inevitably their life will change. We remarked above that only about 3,000 still live as hunter-gatherers. This number must be declining rapidly as the enticement of consumer goods combines with economic discouragement to attract the young to new ways of life — as herdsmen for ranchers, as miners, as trackers for the army, as tourist attractions, as makers of curios, or as servants. The camps do not offer much of a life. They are not a solution.

What we see here is sometimes called ethnocide, or the killing off of a culture. In southern Africa at the present time, ethnocide is a consequence of a failure of policy rather than a deliberate plot of extermination. No one knows quite what to do, given the resources of the area. There were times, in the 19th century, when Bushmen were hunted down and killed as vermin. The danger now is more subtle. A way of life is no longer possible. Can a new way of life be found?

Developmental genocide is easily recognized. It is a fate that has threatened technologically backward peoples since the beginning of history, and hunter-gatherers in particular. In North America, this occurred mainly in the nineteenth century, when the Indians of the great plains were displaced from their hunting grounds by herders and farmers; in South America, this process of displacement continues in Peru, Brazil, Venezuela, Colombia, wherever settlers and plantations, mines and oil wells, new cities and roads are established.

There remain only the forms of hegemonic genocide to consider. Hegemonic genocide is the mass murder of various groups of people in order to force the survivors to submit to the authority of the state. This takes place as part of an attempt to establish, expand or maintain the state. Usually, there has been a crisis: a colonial power has withdrawn, leaving the contenders for power to fight it out among themselves; or the balance of power has changed in such a way that previously submissive groups begin to challenge authority and claim the right to secede. These are the sorts of struggle we see in the disintegration of the federation that used to be Yugoslavia. Mass murders are committed as people are forced to submit to what is left of central authority. How to explain it? The difficulty is that we have layer upon layer of history as group after group has seized power. Each group remembers this history in a time of crisis, and each has reason to fear every other group when the rules of the political game have been destabilized. Now the Croatians, Slovenes, Macedonians, Montenegrans, Albanians, Serbs and Bosnian Muslims all want maximum protection from each other, if not complete independence. If all were in separate territories the whole thing might be settled in a friendly way, after a skirmish or two, but as usual the homogeneous nation-state is a fantasy, shown most clearly in Bosnia-Hercegovina. There, as communist control came to an end, three parties emerged which identified with three national constituencies: a Serbian party (SDS), a Muslim party (SDA) and a Croatian party (HDZ-BiH). Thereafter, each and every important issue became a nationalist issue, capable of dividing the people of Bosnia along national lines, and identified with the nationalist aims of one or other party. Each national group was identified with a different period of domination. Each was "dirty" to the others in a different way.

The Serbians were associated with communist rule; the Croatians with Nazi collaboration during the war; the Muslims with wealth and privileges dating from the Ottoman Empire. The fact that there were communists from all groups, that many Croatians had not collaborated with the Nazis and that most Muslims are as badly off as the next person does not cut any ice in these nationalist fantasies. Parties form to promote the fantasized privileges of the group and the real privileges of the few. That is enough. If someone is to profit, let it be one of ours.

Croatia asserted independence and the European Powers recognized the Croatian claim. This was an immediate threat to the integrity of the Federation, since others began to assert their claims. Why should they not strive to realize their own fantasies? Especially since each of these fantasies was connected to real power? The Muslims were the largest group in Bosnia-Hercegovina (44 % of the total population of the Republic) and made a strong bid for independence. Quite obviously, the Croatians (17%), and the Serbs (35%) were not happy with this. Where did it fit in with their own nationalist aspirations? The result was a bloody war and some episodes of hegemonic genocide, as Serbs and Croats attempted to correct ethnic imbalances by the notorious process of "ethnic cleansing".

Hegemonic wars are a recurrent feature of political transitions. They are occurring in the Soviet Union; they have been particularly associated with the process of decolonization. They become genocidal when it is thought that mere miltary victory will not solve the problem and measures of "population adjustment" are necessary. This may take the form of removing masses of people (as in South Africa under apartheid, when 4 million people were forcibly moved from "white" areas), or may go beyond to the horrors of liquidation. Other tactics may be employed. By killing, a few others may be terrorized into moving voluntarily. When an attempt is made to offer theoretical justification for genocide on a large scale it becomes ideological rather than pragmatic. The preachers of genocide become evangelical rather than furtive. They propose solutions to the world. (We may remark in passing that this was the line of apartheid theorists in their heyday. They did not conceal, they revealed their posture to the world and invited others to imitate them.)

We will include two more forms of genocide: repressive and despotic.

We might use the term "repressive" to refer to politicide (victims distinguished by political affiliation) and the term "hegemonic" to refer to genocide (victims distinguished by race, ethnicity or religion). The test of whether we need two terms rather than one is that they differentiate two processes clearly and consistently. In our sample of case studies, there are two that fall clearly into the hegemonic category: the war against the Ibo secessionists in Nigeria and the war against the Bengali nationalists in Pakistan. Both were struggles with strong ethnic bases and both aroused strong ethnic feelings. Yet the fight against Bengali nationalists might equally well be classed as repressive politicide, since it could be said to be directed against a political group. (For that matter, the fight against Muslims in Bosnia-Hercegovina could be classified either as a fight against the Muslim party SDA or as a fight against Muslims themselves.)

When we turn to Harff and Gurr's 1988 table we find that the Pakistani genocide is classified as repressive/hegemonial. Here is at least one case when it is difficult to tell the difference between repressive politicide and hegemonic genocide. This is not surprising. Political opposition is so often organized around national and ethnic appeals that in striking at a nationalist movement the result is often simultaneously repressive politicide and hegemonic genocide. This impression is strengthened by the frequency with which Harff and Gurr are compelled to use the mixed description hegemonic/repressive. Examples are when governments are massacring Chinese in Malaya (1948-1956), Baluchi tribesmen in Pakistan (1958-1974), Kurdish nationalists in Iraq (1959-75), Moro nationalists in the Philippines (1968-85), Bubi tribesmen in Equatorial Guinea (1969-79), several different tribes in Uganda (1971-79), Bengali nationalists in Pakistan (1971), East Timorese nationalists in Indonesia (1975-present), or Tamil nationalists in Sri Lanka (1983-87). There are also many ambiguous cases among those described simply as repressive: Ukrainian nationalists in USSR (1947-49); Malagasy nationalists in Madagascar (1947-48); Southern nationalists in the Sudan (1952-72); Indians in Guatemala (1966-84); and

Naxalites in India (1968-82).   Are these not hegemonic/-repressive?

There are cases which fit the definition of repressive politicide more clearly. Some of these, such as the Argentinian killing of leftists (1976-80) and the El Salvadorean killing of leftists (1980-90) are more naturally classified as ideological genocides of the Right, whereas others, such as the USSR killing of repatriated nationals (1943-47), are quite naturally classified as ideological genocides of the Left. I would argue that the concept of repressive politicide is not distinctive enough to be retained. We reclassify all instances of repressive genocide as ideological genocide (either revolutionary or conservative), hegemonic genocide, or despotic genocide. We are left with some despotic genocides (in Fein's terminology) to include the last cases of repressive genocide, such as the killing of opponents of the Mobutu regime in Zaire (1977-83). Much of the killing of political opponents in the USSR under Stalin may also be most appropriately classified as despotic — especially the killing of political opponents in the 1930s.

What are "despotic" genocides? They are based on personality cults. Sometimes, in "new" states, artificially held together by personalities rather than principles, unity is achieved by identifying the state with a despot. Naturally, strong measures have to be taken against those who dissent. Without such measures, the state will disintegrate. Yet a moment's reflection will show that this condition is not only true of new states. Europe has provided the clearest examples of both personality cults and despotic leaders imaginable. They are strongly associated with both revolutionary and reactionary ideologies. In fact, wherever some system of ideas is imposed, it is personalized. This is the nature of religion and the nature of salvation politics.

Totalitarian politics are the monologues of a cult figure, speaking sometimes through approved interpreters and sometimes through an "heir". It is Marx or Lenin or Stalin or Hitler or Mussolini who speaks. The first question is always: what does the *Fuehrer* (Leader) say? What is the correct position? Thus, despotism in its most developed form is ideological despotism. Dialogue is as foreign to revolutionary and reactionary ideologies as it is to fundamentalist religions. Dialogue presupposes difference and discovery, incompleteness and change. Revolutionary ideologies aim at one revolution which will be the last one and reactionary ideologies aim at one step backward — also the last.

It is time to summarize. I believe that the classification system which enables us to achieve the maximum resolution with the maximum clarity is the following:

GENOCIDE

IDEOLOGICAL   PRAGMATIC

Progressive   Reactionary   Developmental/Retributive/Hegemonic

We can now list (on the following page) some of the genocides of recent times, adapting Harff and Gurr (1988). This omits the many genocides which occurred during European colonization of the Americas.

IDEOLOGICAL GENOCIDES
(To achieve utopia)

Progressive genocides /politicides
(Towards the "classless" society)

USSR:	kulaks (1929-33)
P.R. China:	class enemies of the Revolution (1950-51; 1966-76)
Ethiopia:	political opposition (1974-79)
N. Vietnam:	rich and middle-class peasants; landlords (1953-54)
Kampuchea:	old regime loyalists, urban dwellers ("bourgeoisie") (1975-79)

Reactionary genocides /politicides
(Towards the "racially pure" state)

Ottoman:	Armenians (1915)
Nazi:	Jews, Gypsies (1940-45)

PRAGMATIC GENOCIDES
(Practical aims: power, domination, revenge)

Developmental genocide
(Eliminating "backward" peoples and their economies)

SWA:	Herero (1904)
USSR:	Chechens, Ingushi, Karachai, Balkars, Kalmycks (1943-57)
Meskhetians:	Crimean Tatars

	(1944-68)
Paraguay:	Ache Indians (1962-72)
Brazil:	Indians of Amazon Basin (continuing)

Retributive genocide /politicide
(Taking revenge)

Rwanda:	Tutsi (1963-64)
Algeria:	Harkis, OAS supporters (1962)
Chile:	leftists (1973-76)

Hegemonic genocide /politicide
(Seizing and holding power)

Burundi:	Hutu (1972)
China:	Taiwanese nationalists (1947)
USSR:	Ukrainian nat/lists (1947-49)
Malaya:	Chinese (1948-56)
Sudan:	southerners (continuing)
Pakistan:	Baluchi tribesmen (1958-74)
P.R. China:	Tibetan nationalists, landowners, Buddhists (1959)
Nigeria:	Ibo living in north (1966)
Pakistan:	Bengali nationalists (1971)
Indonesia:	East Timor nationalists (continuing)
Iran:	Kurds (continuing)
Bosnia:	Muslims (continuing)

This list is not complete and merely demonstrates how the classification system works, so that the reader may judge how informative it is. If the classification of genocide scenarios is to be improved, many examples will have to be studied in detail.

We should also be clear about what a classification of scenarios can achieve and what it cannot. Firstly, there will be a few events which can be classified with accuracy. We can use these as linguists use clear cases to establish the rules of grammar. The fact that there are some clear cases and that we can base our theory on these does not mean that there are not others which are less clear. Some of these are simply mistakes. They are examples of failure and incompetence. They are examples of breakdown. Sentences come out jumbled. We may learn from them if we study the ways in which people try to correct their mistakes. If someone uses the plural incorrectly and then corrects the error, we know that he has a theory about what the correct form should be. We can learn from political theorists in the same way. We hear that they are attempting to achieve a classless society. We may discover that they think that the proper way to a classless society is to level downwards; or that the proper way is to take away wealth from those who have it; or that the proper way is to give everything to the state; or that the proper way is to prevent disagreement and debate. What we try to establish is the "political grammar" of the age and we try to establish it from clear cases, not from the jumble of incompetent performances.

One way to look at the classification of genocides, therefore, is to ask: which are the model cases, the recurring examples which successive genocides appear to imitate?

This is exactly the same question we ask when we look at other varieties of political grammar. When we ask: What is democracy? we look at the models which all are imitating. We discover that there are a couple of models (there are People's Democracies in which no one is allowed to disagree and there are democracies with elections and plenty of argument and real votes and changes of government) and that these models keep recurring.

We could multiply our models of genocide to fit every available case, but this would be a mistake. We would undoubtedly be able to identify a specimen of progressive-reactionary-retributive-developmental-hegemonic genocide. We would merely find ourselves inserting more and more hyphens and complicating the description, as Harff and Gurr themselves found.

Nevertheless, our task for the future will be to collect examples of models, to see whether there are interesting reasons for their success or failure.

This will enable us to sort our way through an enormous amount of detail. It will also prevent us from multiplying our categories beyond what is useful. The fundamental question is: What are people doing and what do they think they're doing? All the other questions flow from this and are secondary.

When we look at the classification of genocides, there is little doubt that in the twentieth century the models for genocide are those of the Nazis and the Soviets. It is no coincidence that they are ideological genocides, with full-blown theories to back them up. Every modern genocide uses some of the vocabulary of these genocides, albeit often in debased form. It depends whether you wish to take a step forward or a step back, whether you wish to be progressive or reactionary, whether you are a modernist or an anti-modernist. Do you wish to embrace all mankind (after it has been purified of counter-revolutionary elements) or do you wish to embrace only the tribe (after it has been purified of all inferior blood)?

Pragmatic genocides are really debased forms of ideological genocides. The actions involved are like those of children who have not yet mastered the grammar of killing. When they are examined, they are either entirely pre-modern or they are weakly justified in terms of progressive or reactionary theory. Nevertheless, it is useful to recognize the practical forms which have been identified in the classification. Several of them can be seen to aspire towards full ideological form, but they fall short in elaboration and correctness. The killing often stops once the goals have been achieved.

The forms which we have identified may be replaced in the future, possibly by patterns which seem relatively benign at the moment. Many political theories seem good when they are first used as weapons against tyranny, but turn out to have disastrous consequences. One of these was the theory of national self-determination. It was used to destroy empires and repressive states. It is being used for that purpose again. But it has had some disastrous consequences. What is the alternative? The alternative is to base the state on a political culture of liberty and pluralism. As we say this, we scan the horizon anxiously for new forms of fundamentalism and authority, for new monologues and new Great Leaders who will utter these monologues. How would we identify a situation with genocidal potential and a revolutionary movement with genocidal inclinations? This is a most important question and one which we shall certainly have to attempt to answer if our book is to be at all useful.

Recognizing genocidal potential

A situation has genocidal potential if there is a genocidal movement and a set of genocidal activators. It is the interaction of the two which is critical. If there is a set of genocidal activators but there is no genocidal movement to take advantage of them, there will be no genocide. The same is true if there is a genocidal movement but the social activators are not present. It will remain a marginal movement of cranks. There are varying degrees of genocide depending on the nature of the movement and the commitment of the activators. A movement which does not have a fully developed theory of genocide is likely to be less thorough than one which does. By "fully developed" we mean that the ideology is a total world view, a theory of history and human destiny.

Such a theory is able to prevent the irruption of distracting ideas (such as a weak humanism, pity, or self-doubt). A fully developed ideology is able to supply the moral consolations of religion. On the other hand, a movement may have the inclination but lack the opportunity. Some genocidal conditions may exist but not others. Let us now list the set of activators and it will be immediately evident that they are cumulative rather than all-or-nothing. This set is inspired by Melson's (1989) comparison of the Armenian genocide and the Holocaust, but we can easily see how the elements of the set recur in the various scenarios proposed above.

Activators of genocidal movements:

* Long history of conflict between perpetrators and victims
* Violent precedents
* Catastrophe and hard times
* Collapse of the centre
* Polarization
* Police unable or unwilling to control paramilitary street violence
* The existing government is regarded as illegitimate
* War

Most of these conditions do not need to be explained. They lead us to search for the history of a conflict and not simply its place in the present. This applies also to apparently spontaneous outbreaks of mob violence. We should remember that a crowd or a mob is merely a poorly defined movement, or a movement in the making, and that its activities are not random.

The conditions also require a government which is no longer respected or obeyed and police and other security forces which are not effective because of this. Often, they have taken sides and are not obeying orders. Finally, major genocides often occur under the cloak of war. This is when fear and hatred are at their peak and when killing is normalized. The vast resources required for genocide can also be mobilized and secrecy maintained where necessary. Genocide can often be presented as a patriotic duty or military necessity during war.

Now we can ask about the genocidal movements which take advantage of these conditions. What are they like and can they be recognized before they come to power? Often, it is difficult to take the perpetrators of genocide seriously until it is too late. They are dismissed as cranks. This is illustrated in a conversation which took place in the early 1930s between a German diplomat and an Italian who was complaining about the lawlessness of the fascists. "Why do you put up with it?" asked the German. "We wouldn't in Germany." The lawless cranks and fanatics of today may become the government of tomorrow unless we learn to recognize and oppose them from the first. The work of Littell (1988) on an early warning system to recognize genocidal movements is a good basis from which to start.

Symptoms of genocidal movements

* Dehumanizing propaganda about target group
* Conspiratorial history. The people have been betrayed
* Utopian ideology. The target group stands between the people and"the good life".
* Politics of polarization pursued and middle ground scorned
* Paramilitary wing; private armies
* Quasi-religious ceremonies of initiation and archaic, secret symbols
* Closed cell organization
* Infiltration and subversion of public institutions
* Young and very young mobilized against the older generation and their parents
* Total loyalty to the movement and its leader
* Violent purges of suspected dissidents

What we have here is a vivid picture of a genocidal movement which is organized to kill the class or race or ethnic group which stands between it and the achievement of utopia. In order to understand it, we should pay careful attention to the content of its ideology. Are ideological enemies redeemable in any way? Can they be converted? Can they be used as slaves? Or are they so dangerous that they should be totally destroyed? What is the theory of history contained in the ideology? Is it a theory of struggle to the death, or a theory in which all who believe will attain salvation?

What is attempted will depend on the exact nature of the core theory and all its ancillary theories and models. What exemplary solutions are spoken of and admired? Who are the heroes of the movement and what are they admired for? What are the most repeated slogans and what do they enjoin people to do? Do they command pitilessness? By means of what sophistries do the intellectuals impose obedience upon themselves? And what image of human being does the movement endorse? Should all be sacrificed to the nation or the state or the cause? Do human beings have value in themselves?

These are the sorts of things which will determine what the movement attempts to do. What it actually achieves will depend on opportunities and the actions of others. The reason why we cannot deliver a predictive theory of society is quite simple. We can summarize it as the strategic dilemma:

> The effect of any move made by any participant in a social/political event will depend on what everyone else does.

The answer is not to be found in the theory of games, since game theory assumes that we know the set of moves. People are continually inventing new moves, much to our consternation. Hitler did not confine himself to the moves that the other German leaders had prescribed for him when they took him into the government in order to control him. In addition to the fact that a social event can be redefined by a clever player, many moves are themselves poorly defined and can be performed cleverly or stupidly. What is it to "argue" with someone or to "reason" with them, or to "plead"? It is not like playing the Jack of spades in bridge. Each of these is an ill-defined move that may have a great effect; similarly, to "brow-beat" or to "threaten" or to "fight". They may be effective or ineffective, depending on the performance not only of the person making the move but also on the performance of all others involved.

These comments are intended to make us cautious in our "science" of politics and genocide. While cautioning against overconfidence though, they are not intended to produce inertia. The very concept of strategic dilemma means that we are encouraged to develop skilled interventions to meet skilled antagonists. Furthermore, even if we cannot rely on predictive science, we can use the method of prediction which is familiar to all observers of the social scene; in other words we can rely on "form".

In many instances, form is quite a good predictor of what will happen if we know the conditions of play. In other cases, the events occur too rarely or the conditions are insufficiently understood or the skills and intentions of the participants are unknown to us. Then we can do little except try our best.

We have gone about as far as we can go with genocide scenarios for the moment. Perhaps we can learn more about genocide by studying the psychology of the people involved. Are they special in some way or are they merely ordinary people? Can psychology tell us anything about the killers and their victims?

CHAPTER SIX

THE SOCIAL PSYCHOLOGY OF GENOCIDE

Furtwängler.: *"Hitler! You do not know the things that are being done in your name."* (Furtwängler's private notes).

Perhaps the most extraordinary fact about the psychology of genocide is that there is no need to search for abnormality. Genocide is the work of perfectly normal and ordinary people, some with a reputation for courage or virtue derived from willingness to sacrifice their feelings in order to carry out a terrible duty on behalf of their people, their class, their cause, or their religion.

The thesis of normality is strongly supported by many cases, but one of the most striking is that described by Christopher Browning in his recent book *Ordinary Men,* a study of the contribution of a reserve police battalion to the massacre of Polish Jews. They were active in the shooting of about 38,000 Jews and the deportation of 45,000 to extermination camps. And when "Jew Hunts" were organized to track down escaped Jews and execute them where found, there were so many volunteers that would-be hunters had to be turned away. Yet these were not specially selected Nazi enthusiasts. They were middle-aged policemen, unfit for regular army service, who had been drafted into a reserve police battalion and posted to Poland. Their commander was distressed by his orders to massacre Jews and offered his men the opportunity to withdraw if they did not feel up to carrying out this duty. Only about a dozen did so immediately and a few did so later on, without any special penalties. How is this to be explained? The first explanation is probably that their commander, Major Trapp, carried out orders in spite of his distress. He set them a splendid example of the triumph of duty. There is no reason to doubt the sincerity of those who later stated that they had wished to do their duty and not leave everything to their comrades. They did not wish to seem "cowardly" or too "weak" to answer the call of the Fatherland. And would it have helped if they had not done the job? Someone had to do it and undoubtedly would have done it. Most of these ordinary men suffered, to some extent. Neither should we neglect the fact that to some, the special duties of organized massacre and of hunting down Jews were exciting. Perhaps the comment which tells us most is: "Truthfully, I must say that, at the time, we didn't reflect on it at all". Each of us has had that experience. We have not reflected on things we have done. If we have had the good fortune to live prosperously in a moderately decent society then we will have avoided the worst excesses purely by chance. Only rarely do people transcend the conventional standards of their times. Those who have grown up in racist or sexist societies find it very difficult to explain, when circumstances have changed, how they could have discriminated so easily and unquestioningly against the disadvantaged. Even the brightest and the best often find that they have been patronizing and thoughtless.

Let us illustrate tragic normality yet once again with a short biography of a petty official in the Nazi Party, Herr Neisse, the gardener described by Christabel Bielenberg (1984).

He has become the *Blockwart*, or Party representative for the immediate neighbourhood. He sends in reports on those who do not behave patriotically, collects subscriptions, sells postcards and pamphlets for Party funds. During the week he is a gardener; on Sundays he wears a brown uniform. He is "resurgent Germany". What are the outlines of his story? He had returned to Berlin and the girl he intended to marry after the sudden and suprising defeat of Germany in 1918. One moment there was talk of great victories being won and the next — defeat! He and his intended both worked for a pittance to save enough to get married, but suddenly came the first of the economic catastrophes — the inflation of 1923 — reducing their savings to virtually nothing. All that he could afford to buy was a cup and saucer for Hilde, his intended. He had no doubt that there had been a plot; in any case, his confidence in the Weimar government was shaken — as was his confidence in himself, since he was apparently not a man who could earn enough to get married. Nevertheless, a man must live and the two of them struggled to their feet again, battling against unemployment. In another five years, when he was nearly forty, he had saved enough for a garden allotment and felt that he was able to marry. During this period he had noticed, so he said, a change in the suburb where he did his gardening. The respectable Germans were replaced by Jews and shopkeepers (whom he called "white Jews"). He and Hilde saved to buy half a share in a vegetable stall, hoping to take a minute step up the social ladder, when the hyperinflation of 1929 commenced. Who was responsible for this new catastrophe? The national socialists seemed to have the answer: International Jewry. It was a conspiracy of International Jewry and the only ones who were taking steps to counter their moves were the Nazis. They were looking after the ordinary man, they were fighting for the honour of Germany against the dishonour inflicted at Versailles. They were not kissing the arses of International Jewry. ("No, not any particular Jew. Many of them are harmless. International Jewry").

Neisse joined the Party in 1931; when Hitler became Chancellor in 1933 he was rewarded for his regular attendance at Party meetings and payment of Party dues by being made *Blockwart*. He loved Hitler. When the vulgarities and extravagances of the Party elite were noticed, his answer was that Hitler did not know these things. (This is also what communists in the Soviet Union said of Stalin during the worst of the purges, as Eugenia Ginzburg tells us in her book *Into the Whirlwind*. If only someone would let Stalin know what was happening!) Herr Neisse was not alone in this. Carl Goerdeler, at that time *Reichskommissar* for prices and mayor of Leipzig (and later one of the leaders in the unsuccessful assasination attempt on Hitler in 1944), was a concerned German who attempted to influence British policy towards Germany in the late 1930s. Waley, a British Treasury official with whom Goerdeler had contact, noted his views. Hitler was innocent; German policy was shaped by Nazi Party bosses; if they could be removed, Hitler would be all right. To others, Goerdeler said that the opposition (mainly the army) could liquidate the SS and that Hitler might then be kept on as "President in a gilded cage" without significant powers (Ludlow,1986, p.145). All sorts of people related to Hitler because he was so obviously sincere and homely, a simple soldier who did his duty for love of Germany. He was not up to the plotting and vicious opportunism of Himmler and Goering and all the others. But people had confidence that he would win through.

When Mrs Bielenberg returned to Berlin in 1946 she was told that Herr Neisse had been hanged from a lamppost, though no one knew who had done it. Perhaps the best comment is a cruel joke she tells at the begining of her story of Herr Neisse: When Hitler was born, three good fairies made him their promises. The first promised that every German should be honest, the second that every German should be intelligent, the third that every German should be a Nazi. Then came the bad fairy and announced that no one could have more than two of these qualities. Herr Neisse may have been one of the honest Nazis, but even his worst enemies could not have accused him of intelligence.

We have looked at two examples. In the first, ordinary men participated in genocide. In the second, an ordinary man joined a party which promoted the idea of genocide. At first the genocidal intentions of the party were not clear to most members, but what was completely clear from the start was that the party would act violently to expel Jews from the normal life of Germany and would strip them of their citizenship. And when we turn to other examples of violence, we find again that perfectly ordinary, sane people can be brought to participate. They may participate in the planning of nuclear war or the development of weapons of unimaginable power which could destroy all human life. They can bomb people they have never seen and destroy men, women and children. They can carry out holy wars. They can be trained as terrorists.

Here is a final example of incitement to virtuous killing. David Hirst (1992) describes a visit to the emir of a Salvation mosque in a Cairo suburb. He is received with courtesy and wonders whether "this slight, bespectacled, mild mannered young man in his white robe" can be "one of those 'Islamic terrorists' who are murdering Christians to the south in Upper Egypt, assassinating 'apostates' in the capital, and threatening the stability of the most important country in the Arab world?" He listens to a sermon which is an impassioned call to the people to rise up against their 'heathen oppressors'. The aim of the growing movement — the Islamic Association — is to restore "the sovereignty of God" on Earth. And the movement does not only talk. There have been assassinations, sanctioned by quotations from the Koran. The emir, Mohammed Gayid, is a believer and he is implacable. He believes in a holy war against the heathen. To understand him, one needs to consider both the political tradition which he has inherited and the strategic choices which he has made to solve his personal problems. He is an unemployed graduate of a college of irrigation in a country of 3 million unemployed graduates. Who can be to blame? What is the solution for this crisis? One way of dealing with a problem is to treat it as a purely personal matter and suffer in private. Another is to politicize it and convert it into a matter of concern for hundreds of thousands. This is possible if the misery is widespread and a telling political story can be told; most important, if there are strategists who can convert a political story into successful political action. The emir has succeeded in making a political story of his private problems. They will be solved by a holy war in which those who have plotted the misery of Islam will be eliminated.

We can't explain genocide (and other kinds of political violence) in terms of psychological abnormality. It has never been necessary to empty the lunatic asylums in order to recruit people for pogroms or genocides or holy wars. Then how should we explain it? The first possibility is that behaviour is a product of social situations. After all, isn't that what we have seemed to suggest so far? What can social psychologists tell us about patterns of social behaviour?

When we turn to what I call "minimalist social psychology", we find some useful hints, but we soon realize that we have to make many assumptions as we string them together to form a plausible story. What do I mean by minimalist social psychology? It is the sort of psychology which demonstrates that certain social effects can be produced by minimal means. Take a few people who have never met before, give them the minimum of context, put them together for the minumum amount of time, and see whether they will form groups, be obedient to the instructions of the experimenter, produce norms of behaviour, learn good and bad conduct by action or from example, fill in questionnaires in ways which seem to measure prejudice and personality, attribute properties to each other in ways which indicate that they are sensitive to context, and respond to a variety of forms of influence and power.

Like minimalist art, it has its admirers: the wonder of it is that we can discern the lineaments of society through the smudges of method. We discover that persons will form groups on the basis of whether they are supposed to be admirers of Kandinsky or Klee and that accepting such a classification is enough to produce mild forms of in-group preference; that they will often alter their reported judgements in order to conform to a majority but that sometimes a minority can swing the majority around by sticking to its guns; that most people will obey even outrageous instructions once they have accepted an authority; that people often prefer to remain bystanders and not get involved (usually under rather obvious conditions; more interesting is the fact that people of some cultures and subcultures do get involved in particular issues; no one ever gets involved in everything); that there are different tactics for expressing prejudice, some of them less direct than others (so-called "modern" or "subtle" expressions of prejudice often replace good old-fashioned direct statements of hatred); that the victim is often blamed on the "just world" principle that people get what they deserve; that some people are more given to identify with authority and be hostile to outsiders than others. People most apt to accept authority appear to have three measurable characteristics: submission to authority, as in "It is always better to trust the judgement of the proper authorities in government or religion"; conventionalism, as in "It may be considered old-fashioned by some, but having a decent, respectable appearance is still the mark of a gentleman and, especially, a lady"; and agression towards outsiders as in "Once our government leaders and authorities condemn the dangerous elements in our society, it will be the duty of every patriotic citizen to help stamp out the rot that is poisoning our country from within".

We find also that there are different forms of power (we may coerce, we may persuade, using the media and other organs, we may impose ourselves as legitimate authorities who have the right to give orders, we may pass ourselves off as experts, with or without justification, or we may solve emotional problems for the group, such as the emotional problem of self-respect).

The difficulty in each case is that we do not know how general the conclusions should be, for two simple reasons. The first is that minimalist theories neglect culture. Not only culture in general, but the specific culture of the situation in which the person is trying to make sense of things. If we hope to know what people will do in particular situations, we have to know what they think the rules of the game are. Do they think that the rule of the game is "mind your own business and do as you are told" (in a given situation), or do they think that the rule is "see how many loopholes you can find and how often you can disagree with everybody else"? Culture, to put it baldly, enables us to see a particular event as a situation to which certain rules apply.

The second reason why minimalist theories go wrong is that they do not include the full context in which people act. Since our experiments usually restrict opportunities for interpretation we tend to recreate them on the basis of experience. We are likely to be wrong. We are certainly wrong if we believe that persons are indifferent to social contexts or do not try to make tactical decisions within the limits imposed by their understanding of the situation. Illustrations from minimalist social psychology can be of value when used to exhibit prejudice and power, as well as the ease with which conformity, obedience and group membership may be produced. They cannot predict what will happen in society, but they can be used to show how events might plausibly turn out, as we shall see.

What we should realize is that the schema for interpreting every action is:

> who
> does what
> with whom
> where and when

> for what purpose
> with what consequences
> according to what rules (culture)
> in what societal context

Often, we can make a fair guess at the rules. It is only when we operate as theorists that we get it wrong, because we are impelled by the rigour of our theory to reach the wrong conclusion for the right reasons.

The only social scientists who have a slight chance of understanding social situations or of giving correct advice are those who realize that people are strategists (though frequently very bad strategists) and that to understand them we have to understand their strategies in a societal context. To attempt to understand strategies is much more useful than to attempt to grasp the "laws" of psychology. We will then realize why results are so predictable in some situations and unpredictable in others. Where they are predictable, it is because we understand the culture and the situation in which people are making decisions. Where they are unpredictable, it is because we do not know the culture and the situation. By a "situation" we mean the context of society, or of institutions and societal processes. Have we not all experienced changes in understanding as we are fed information about the societal context of an apparently mad and chaotic action? (Reicher,1987.)

Suppose that mob violence has occurred in which someone has been hacked and necklaced. At first, the whole event seems to be a crazy incident in which a primitive mob went out of control and behaved in a frenzied and irrational way. Then you discover that the person necklaced was a particularly brutal official. Then you hear that he had raped a young girl in the township. Then you hear that on the day of the necklacing a number of women had been to his house to protest about his behaviour and tell him to stop molesting young girls. Then you hear that he was abusive and unrepentant. The women were joined by others who also reproached him with working for the apartheid government. He then locked the door of his house and fired a shot at the crowd through a window, wounding someone; and so on.

What we have here is a situation which does not develop mechanically from first confrontation to killing, but rather develops decision by decision in a context of tense and prolonged opposition between ordinary people and government officials. If conflicts like these are repeated, people begin to behave in similar ways, and we can speak of the beginnings of a culture, a set of beliefs and rules about how to behave in such situations. As events become intelligible we see the persons involved behaving like rational actors rather than like automata following laws. But this sort of thing is bad news for the stripped-down version of psychology. If we should try to understand human behaviour as strategic action in culture and situation, then we should also reconsider the elements of psychological explanation.

Look at the following. What do some crucial decisions of the *Joodsche Raad* or Jewish Council in Holland, decisions of Dietrich Bonhoeffer, and those of Adolf Eichmann have in common? All were persuaded by Nazi strategy to make minute distinctions which furthered Nazi aims. All were persuaded to make distinctions (for very different reasons) between Jews to be protected and other Jews. Eichmann protested: "I did not know that Jews from the Reich evacuated to the East were subject to the same treatment. That is what I did not know". Bonhoeffer attempted, for tactical reasons, to protect baptized Jews rather than all Jews (von Klemperer, 1986). The *Joodsche Raad* in Holland was under the impression that only German and other foreign Jews would be deported; hence they cooperated with the SS in creating a Jewish police force (Arendt,1963). From the first, Nazi strategy aimed at dividing and controlling people. Firstly, Jews were divided from the rest of the population by having to wear yellow stars. Then Nazi policy appeared to distinguish between local and foreign Jews and in this way the collaboration of Jewish Councils and Jewish police was secured. After all, wouldn't it be better for the victims if they administered their own affairs and made their own selections? This was a strategy to which the only effective counter was to refuse to make distinctions.

Each of the events described above can only be understood strategically, as a contest between parties making up the rules of play in a situation which unfolds unpredictably. We can learn certain moves, we can study strategies, but we cannot assume that they will always work. The game changes. A psychology stripped of culture and strategy has little hope of coming to terms with the complexities of political decisions. If we find social psychology, as currently used in its minimalist form, to be largely useless in understanding genocide and other political events, what is the alternative? The best solution, it appears, is to try to construct a social psychology based on people acting in the context of their cultural and institutional settings. The essentials of such a setting would entail, for the political psychologist, a description of culture and its transformation in strategic contexts by persons acting as members or opponents of political movements.

Social psychology of politics

What are the elements of a social psychology of politics — one which would enable us to understand events such as genocide?

The first is culture. People act within a set of assumptions or rules. They act with a certain know-how and they act with theories of history and society and identity. They have to know how they relate to other people. Their culture is not static. It is, in fact, hotly contested and fast-changing. When there is a continuity of culture we can speak of a tradition. When there is not, we may speak of a cultural revolution and of a new tradition.

The second important basic ingredient of an approach to political psychology is the concept of a movement. People join movements, or create movements, or support movements. Movements are the social units of action in politics. Individuals are effective through movements, because politics is a mass activity. Movements are essential for the ideological transformation of reality. Communist movements, fascist movements, Nazi movements, democratic movements and nationalist movements are movements to secure political power and achieve ideological transformation of the social world.

The third important ingredient of political psychology is the psychodynamics and cognitive functioning of leaders and followers.

In particular, we are interested in the process by which their private ambitions, miseries and pleasures are politicized and transformed into public concerns. The process by which this occurs can be termed ideological acceleration and transformation. The world is ideologically tranformed by persons who have themselves been ideologically transformed and separated from others.

Our task in trying to understand the social psychology of genocide is to understand it in terms of a general political psychology. That is, we have to understand human behaviour within the context of political movements which occupy various niches in the social system. A political movement is a group of people who attempt to gain power, either by acting within an established political tradition or by creating a revolutionary tradition.

Let us now examine each of the three components of the theory of political psychology in turn.

Political Culture of Genocide

Since we are particularly interested in genocide, I shall confine most of my remarks to genocidal culture. Furthermore, I shall take Nazi Germany as my main example, simply on the principle of searching where the light is brightest. "Brightness" refers here to the bright light of scholarship, not to the bright light of the subject.

A political culture has a number of ingredients, some of which are listed below.

> *ideas, theories,ways of talking ("discourses")
> *ways of doing things ("practices")
> *models of government
> *rules of behaviour (and morals)
> *images, myths, histories

When we analyze a genocidal culture and its relation to previously existing political cultures, we should show which of these elements are transformed.

German anti-semitism took the form of talk, theories of Jewish racial characteristics, popular theories of the secret world conspiracy of Jews, and images of Jews as enemies of the Christian religion. It was carried in what Staub (1989;1990) calls the "deep structure" of the culture, ready to be revived in spite of the fact that Jews had gained full civic rights at the time of the unification of Germany and the establishment of the German Reich in 1871.

The Nazi movement made use of this existing culture of anti-semitism and then intensified it as well as linking it to other theories. They pursued the implications of the view that Jews were responsible for Germany's defeat and linked this with the theory that there was an international conspiracy of Jews, acting both as capitalists and bolsheviks, from the right and from the left. They intensified the prejudice against Jews as defectives and dirty disease carriers and linked this with a theory of racial hygiene which enabled them to draw in scientists and doctors to assist in the task of purifying the nation. Their extermination programme would henceforth be more than an act of political expediency; it would be an action motivated by scientific and technical considerations of the highest order, directed at terminating unworthy life and improving the health of the nation. It would therefore include gypsies and Slavs and other subhumans. The linking of genocide and "positive eugenics" was a powerful theoretical move, since it disarmed those liberals and visionary socialists who thrived on "progressive" science (Weindling,1990). Hitler was seen as the man who had the will to put into practice the medical vision of which others were still dreaming. National socialism was the future! Theory must of course become practice if it is to have any results, and at the level of practice, the Nazis began their experiments in mass murder with mental defectives and gradually included "subhuman races". In the occupied territories they progressed from clubbing, shooting and hanging to machine-gunning and finally the setting up of death camps where killing could be both medicalized and industrialized. Hence the bizarre phenomenon of the "Nazi doctors" studied by Lifton (1986). Doctors had to apply their "medical" knowledge to the sorting of victims arriving at the death camps into those fit for labour and those to be immediately exterminated. Doctors were there to perform bizarre experiments as well as to look after the health of the inmates and sign the death certificates. Doctors played their role in studying methods of killing.

Brute prejudice had come a long way since the cries immediately after the First World War that Germany had been stabbed in the back by Jews and that the way to take revenge was to destroy them or use them as hostages to threaten world Jewry. By 1920 an associate of Hitler's, Hans Knodn, had written a proposal on interning all Jews and expelling them from Germany. Hitler had himself written in *Mein Kampf* that the gassing of 12-15,000 Jews would have improved German morale wonderfully during the war (Strauss,1988).

The Nazis had to develop an entirely new model of government to deal with "the Jewish problem". First, they had to deprive Jews of their citizenship. Secondly, they had to introduce the *Fuehrer* principle: the basis of law was the will of the *Fuehrer*, which had to be interpreted by other leaders, each in charge of some segment of the German state. The implication is that genocide may have started in various ways at various times in different parts of the system as leaders struggled to be first in interpreting Hitler's will. Raul Hilberg believes that the decision to destroy Russian Jews was taken earlier than the decision to destroy the rest of Europe's Jews. By August 1941 Hitler had given Himmler and Heydrich the "green light" to draw up an extermination plan for the rest of Europe's Jews and by October, a mere two months later, implementation of the plan had begun.

Rules of behaviour and morals changed. The summit of decency was now loyalty and obedience to the *Fuehrer* rather than obedience to one's conscience. Furthermore, it was the race that counted, not the individual. Finally, one had to steel oneself to murder in order to improve the health of the race. Medical killing meant the transformation of the medical ethic from its primary purpose of caring for the patient to that of caring for the race, a patient that could only be treated by killing human "microbes".

Even the Church cooperated. In a collection of letters, diaries and documents (Klee, Dressen and Riess, 1992) we can follow the visit of two senior army chaplains (acting on a complaint by yet two other chaplains) to 90 Jewish children whose parents had recently been executed. The children were thirsty and starving. The chaplains were dismayed by the conditions under which the children were being kept and by the fact that their wailing could be heard by both soldiers and civilians. Such things should not take place in the public eye, they felt. After an investigation, the commander of the Sixth Army, Field Marshall von Reichenau, ordered that the execution of the children should proceed. The Church offered little resistance. The execution was carried out by the local Ukrainian militia who fired so badly that many children had to be shot several times.

What is clear from this is that the Nazi movement succeeded in radically transforming the political culture of Germany at all levels. It changed ideas, practices, rules of behaviour, models of government and society, and theories of history.

My purpose here is to use this as an illustration of the way in which we have to start to explain genocide. We have to understand the culture which the genocidal movement exploits and transforms for its purposes. And we have to understand culture as a set of rules and techniques for doing things.

Now we examine the second component of the theory of political psychology — the role of movements.

Genocidal Movements

A movement is a group of people who act together (some of the time — no collection of people is in complete harmony) to achieve a political aim. They want to take over the government or influence the government.

A movement consists of leaders, followers, critics and sympathizers. It may claim either the living or the dead as patrons and embodiments of the ideals of the movement. And every movement has a political culture. If it wants to do something it has to have a set of plans formulated within a set of assumptions about what society should be. Should society do more for women? or workers? or minorities? or the free market? Should it do less for white males? capitalists? Chinese? Naturally, in order to accomplish these things it has to have some notion about how society as a whole should be organized.

Every society has within it a number of movements which differ from each other in many ways. One of these ways is their use of violence to achieve their aims. Every society has movements which range from genocidal to pacifist, with others somewhere in between. The in-between movements believe in tit for tat, or limited violence to achieve their aims and defend themselves, whereas genocidal movements believe that they can defend themselves and achieve their goals only by complete elimination of a defined enemy.

This proposition may be greeted with incredulity by those who live in tranquil societies. Where are our genocidal movements? they will ask. The answer is that the would-be perpetrators of genocides belong to fringe movements of cranks while a society is stable and prosperous. Nevertheless, they exist. They emerge rapidly during troubled times, or when the government appears to be betraying its followers, or when there is a power vacuum. They also emerge when a country is conquered by like-minded people and they are offered an opportunity to put their theories into practice. The Nazis found genocidal collaborators wherever they went.

The proposition here is that the emergence of genocide is a problem of social ecology. The potential is there. Just as particular species which have previously been insignificant begin to spread when the environment is right for them, so genocidal movements become a menace when conditions are right. The Nazis were a fringe movement of "cranks" who would have been totally insignificant in a prosperous society. If this hypothesis is correct, it explains why the people who commit genocide are not abnormal and can very rarely be classified as mentally ill. They are the normal members of a political movement acting in an unstable and threatening social environment. They are often evil and repulsive, but they are sane.

I discuss the social ecology of genocide in the chapter on genocide scenarios: the collapse of legitimate authority; the existence of groups which have been enemies for a long time; precedents of victimization; the existence of histories and theories which explain this hostility; shortages, unemployment and economic decline; military defeat; war. It is not difficult to understand why parties of violence should emerge during times of catastrophe. Genocidal parties have a particular appeal since they clearly identify the enemy and attribute responsibility for the anxiety and sufferings which people are experiencing. They are seldom inventive. They do not need to stretch the imagination since the chosen victims are those who have always been the enemies. What gives the genocidal movement its freshness is ritual and some new theories to justify an old sentiment.

No matter how favourable an environment is for a particular movement, leadership is a critical factor in success. Both Hitler and Lenin (among many other revolutionary leaders), were prepared to make bold moves. As we saw in the chapter on the Holocaust, Hitler refused to join the government except on his own terms, even though the electoral popularity of the Nazis was on the wane. He would be Chancellor or nothing. He became Chancellor.

Lenin's role in the October revolution also shows us how important leadership is to the success of a movement. It was he who defined the situation in Russia as revolutionary when other bolshevik leaders believed that they would have to wait for a long time to launch a successful revolution. Their theory was that February had seen a "bourgeois-democratic" revolution and that a long period of time would have to elapse before Russia was ready for a socialist revolution. They were blinded by theory. Lenin diagnosed the situation as revolutionary because it had three essential characteristics. There was confusion in the policy of the rulers; there had been an unusual increase in the sufferings of the oppressed classes; and, as a consequence, there had been a rise in the level of mass action. When he arrived in Petrograd in April 1917 he set about redefining the situation for the revolutionary movement under the slogan "All power to the Soviets!" Prior to that, he had been responsible for a number of crucial strategic decisions. He had redefined party membership so as to include only activists, splitting the party into bolsheviks (who followed his line) and Mensheviks (who followed the softer line of Martov). This small party of dedicated revolutionaries was able to resist the Okhrana, or Tsarist secret police. Then, he had insisted that revolutionaries were to be found among all classes and rejected the idea of a separate proletarian movement or class culture, even if he continued to believe that class conflict was the dynamo of history. On its own, the working class was only capable of developing trade union consciousness. Hence a party of revolutionaries was essential. Finally, he formulated the idea of the party-state system which meant that a single party should exist and rule. Apart from these decisions of grand strategy, there were many moments when crucial tactical moves turned events. The most notorious of these was the termination of the sittings of the Constituent Assembly. The elections, which had been arranged by Kerensky before his downfall, were a disaster for the bolsheviks, who won fewer than a quarter of the seats. But they had tactically important majorities in Petrograd and Moscow. The Constituent Assembly was closed when a guard marched in and announced: "The guard is tired". Apparently, the elective representatives were equally tired. They retired. The Assembly was never reopened, though representatives did make some attempts to meet again. They could formulate no plans to resist the bolshevik coup.

Now it is time to discuss the third component of the social psychology of politics — the ways in which private miseries are politicized.

CHAPTER SEVEN

PSYCHODYNAMICS AND IDEOLOGICAL TRANSFORMATION

"The supreme sacrifice is to become evil in the service of a greater good and commit the evil deed that is truly and tragically moral." (Boris Savinkov)

What interests us here is the process by which private miseries, conflicts and deprivations come to be seen as collective miseries, conflicts and deprivations. The sufferer joins a group and what was private becomes public when experience is collectivized and ideologized. People create theories and movements to achieve this. Feminists ideologized the private miseries of many women — their inferior pay, their lack of educational opportunities, their inferior status in law — and made a collective issue of what had previously been purely personal experiences of unhappiness.

This process is best called ideological transformation. It is the process by which personal experience becomes collective experience, and is one of the main functions of joining a movement.

Children may experience conflicts about love and power and develop ways of resolving them which may then be transformed into ideological commitments in adolescence and early adulthood and expressed in political action. Sometimes the results are cranky, since personal conflicts may be be ideologized as a belief in the occult, or astrology, or attachment to some fringe movement. From time to time this is innovative and important; often it is heavy work to make social issues of them. When the original conflicts energize ideologies that are metaphors of developmental problems, there can be no guarantee that the ideologies will address important social issues. Sometimes they do, and then the ideologue solves a personal and a social problem at the same time, experiencing certainty and exaltation. The power of such solutions is felt when it turns out that they are general, and that the innovator has solved the problems of a generation. Such are "world-historical" individuals. By ideologizing developmental problems they can be resolved on the stage of history. Individual and social development seem to work in tandem and people experience the exhilaration of new ideas and inner liberation.

This is not reductionist. Developmental conflicts do not account for ideologies; they account merely for some of the energy and enthusiasm with which people attach themselves to ideology. It is reasonable to ask: What personal identity problems are being resolved by those individuals who belong so entirely and uncritically to a given movement? We may also ask: What is the source of repetitive and maladaptive behaviours which show up from time to time in different leaders? We do not account for the whole process of transformation — that still has to be explained — and we do not account for the ideology — that has its own history; but we mark the kernel of the conflict which is transformed and the vitality of its reincarnation as an ideological commitment.

Ideological transformation is the first process by which the private becomes public. It occurs when an individual encounters or creates an ideology which shows that a personal problem is in fact a common problem. The theoretical component of the ideology will explain the world in more or less grand terms, the action component will usually prescribe joining a particular movement in order to overcome particular opponents, and the moral component will show the person why it is right to do so.

We now come to the second part of the process, which is ideological acceleration. The analogy here is the centrifuge. When substances are placed in a centrifuge the high speed of rotation separates them. We observe an analogous process during ideological acceleration. People take a series of steps as they join groups, say things which commit them more and more strongly to the movement and are separated more and more completely from others outside the group. Gentiles who had Jewish friends now hate Jews; people who do not know a capitalist from a concrete mixer believe that capitalists have to be eliminated; and when the accelerator is working properly, instant classes may be created and separated, as Xianling tells us in his book *Half of Man is Woman*. Intellectuals, right wing deviationists, reformists and reform reformists can be instantly created and separated from the body of the movement.

In the movement, ideological acceleration takes the form of a sequence of actions which take you into faster and faster lanes. Each acceleration is the result of an action which removes you further from people at the centre. The sequence consists of acts of increasingly violent contempt for outsiders. It may start with words and uniforms and end in killing. In between, there have been oaths of loyalty, hate slogans, acts of damage to property, humiliations inflicted on enemies and grand processions. A combination of rewards and punishments, of conviviality and terror, is used to define the movement and attach members to it. But the pressure is always to take the next step of commitment. For those who have gone a certain way, there is the pressure not to retreat. The pressure to take the next step frequently takes the form of rewards. Just as frequently the pressure not to retreat takes the form of punishment and terror.

The right and the assumed capacity to define utopia and separate the good from the bad are the crucial properties of the complete ideological accelerator. The most complete separation is always moral, as is the most perfected system of terror. The ideological accelerator is always a moral accelerator, finally splitting the world into two hostile camps. Now we can see where the ideological accelerator leads: it leads to utopia. In more ambitious times, it leads to heaven. Only the bravest have the courage to refuse to climb that ladder. One such was the Haitian chief, Hatuey, who was offered baptism before being burnt alive. Galeano (1989) reports the conversation between him and his tormentors in *Memory of Fire*. "Are there Christians in that heaven?" he asked. "Yes," they assured him eagerly. "Then let me go to hell," he replied. Too few seem to ask that question of the framers of utopia: "Are there many like you in your utopia?"

The psychological consequences of this moral process are not difficult to conjecture. The world is split in such a way that those who are victimized deserve what they get. How infinitely preferable a sporadically immoral system would be! The casual vice of murderers and mercenaries is so much more decent than the systematic vice of utopians! I am in favour of intelligent and humble sceptics who are unlikely ever to gain power.

An outline of a typical process of ideological transformation and acceleration would illustrate some of the things we have been discussing. Naturally, this is merely one of the possible paths which the process might follow and could vary from case to case.

IDEOLOGICAL TRANSFORMATION AND ACCELERATION

SOCIAL EVENTS	PSYCHOLOGICAL EVENTS
Catastrophe	*Insecurity*
Unemployment, etc.	*Fear and anger; search for cause*
Movement explains	*Interested*
Movement blames	*Even more interested*
Movement humiliates those "responsible"	*Excited, pleased*
Movement rewards those who join	*Seriously interested*
Rallies, activities	*Join*
Violence: movement shows strength	*Impressed*
Political successes	*Respectable now*
Serious action against those "undermining the state"	*Split world into good/bad*
Genocide	*The bad were a lot worse than one knew*

106

The table is, I hope, self-explanatory. Persons who join any movement are engaged in a certain amount of ideological trans- formation and acceleration, or of division of the world into deserving insiders and less deserving outsiders. We know, thanks to the experiments of Tajfel (1978) that, even without a scale of increasing rewards and punishments such as would be used by movements and organizations in the real world, people can form groups merely by being categorized as similar in some way, and that they then allocate more goods to insiders than to outsiders. We also know that when people join groups or are placed in groups, they are strongly influenced by the group culture. Everyone who has been a member of an army unit will know how strong the culture of obedience is and how difficult it is to disobey even clearly illegitimate orders. Young soldiers can become torturers if they are commanded to torture by superior officers and are surrounded by young men who have already complied. The strongly reinforced culture of obedience, the close interdependence of men together in danger, the fact that killing is normal in war, and ever-present fear make it easier to obey than to disobey — often leading to further and even grosser acts. We know from the experiments of Milgram that even the minimal pressure of believing that one is participating in an experiment is enough to make most people inflict punishment amounting to torture (Milgram, 1974). The conclusions drawn about the prop- er way to behave in common situations constitute the group cul- ture. This is how the process of ideological acceleration shapes movements. This is what makes us go beyond the orders given to prove our zeal. We learn quickly how to extrapolate once we have accepted and been accepted.

Leaving the ideological accelerator

We are frequently tempted to take a mechanical view of events.When we discover the conditions under which people form groups we would like to say that whenever these conditions are present, people will form groups as predicted. Yet our predictions depend entirely on whether or not persons accept the implicit and explic- it culture of the situation. If they are participating in an experi- ment, we depend on their accepting the rules of the experiment. What happens if they challenge these rules? What happens if they start with a point of view which is diametrically opposed to our experiment? We know by now that disagreement when we are attempting to impose uniformity will immediately call the prevailing assumptions into question. Minorities can have a strong influence on decisions if they stick to their guns (Moscovici,1985; Mugny,1982). This is exactly what we expect when we adopt a strategic rather than a mechanical view of social processes. In every social event there are choices. People are usually aware of alternatives and start with different points of view. Our picture of the process of ideological acceleration (or of any other process leading from psychological condition A to condition B) should allow for differences in point of view and for competing influences. The appropriate picture is not mechanical, it is strategic, argumentative, or even conversational (Du Preez,1980). People talk to each other, or communicate in other ways, and as a result they have the capacity, limited though it may be by their past and their appreciation of the present, to change their minds.

We may use this to understand the Resistance in Germany. There were those, such as convinced communists, social democrats and a minority of Christians, who opposed the Nazis from the beginning. There were others, such as romantic conservatives and nationalists who accepted the Nazis at first and then later opposed them. There were yet others who went all the way with the Nazis.

Though it would be interesting to trace in some detail the tactics followed by those who never joined, we shall confine this account to those who started the process of joining and then withdrew. There were many, both known and unknown. This group includes many of the figures who featured in the bomb plot of 20 July 1944 which attempted to kill Hitler by planting a bomb in his field headquarters.

Let us take von Stauffenberg as representative, since he was the man who actually planted the bomb. At first, like others, he welcomed the coming of Hitler. The Nazis were all in favour of removing the restrictions of the Versailles treaty, doing away with reparations and re-arming Germany. Stauffenberg was attracted to the *Volkisch* ideal, or "the ideal of a community of the people, united and working for the common good

(Hoffmann, 1970, p. 317). Von Stauffenberg and his brothers "agreed in principle with the idea of control, separate existence and the essentially foreign non-German character of the Jews, though they objected to extremism and physical cruelty" (Ibid. p. 318). He was an aristocrat and Hitler was a petit-bourgeois — "the wallpaper hanger" was one expression he used. Yet even as late as 1938 he was in favour of the removal of Jews from German cultural life. Like many others he revised his opinion of Hitler after the stunning successes of the Polish and the French campaigns. ("That man's father was not a petit-bourgeois; that man's father is war.") He changed his mind again when Hitler invaded Russia — many in the army saw it as a strategic calamity — and he was horrified by the barbarous conduct of the war and the mass murders of Jews and other civilians. But what did he stand for? He wanted the army to take over and restore the old Germany of "natural ranks", a Germany in which the nobility would play a significant role. It is not surprising, after the apparent success of the Nazis in wooing the masses, that even social democrats wished to restrict mass democracy. Certainly, Stauffenberg had no enthusiasm for the Left, for socialism or trade unions. Nevertheless, the plan was to include two social democrats (Julius Leber, who held out under Gestapo torture for two weeks while the Hitler assassination plot was going forward and Wilhelm Leuschner, prominent as a labour leader) in the coup government. All of them were compromised in one way or another. Not one of them was enthusiastic about "mass democracy", for reasons which are understandable in the context of the time, and none of them made realistic proposals for a democratic postwar Germany. One reason why so few left wing leaders were included was that many had been killed and the Communist Party had been thoroughly infiltrated by the Gestapo. An accurate count is not yet possible, but between 100,000 and 200,000 members of the Left were arrested in the Third Reich (Mason, 1986).

One way to interpret the plot was that it was a mere rebellion of conservative elites who had lost influence; when they saw things going badly, they tried to get rid of Hitler. This interpretation suggests that there was no moral dimension to their action; but it ignores the courage required to move from passive disapproval of Hitler and the Nazis to active opposition. All knew that they would probably have to pay a terrible price. It is more likely that the officers who joined the plot had at first accepted parts of the Nazi vision and been overwhelmed by Hitler's achievements before becoming morally or opportunistically opposed to Hitler. There can be little doubt that some members of the Resistance were morally outraged from the beginning (von Trott, Bielenberg, von Moltke), whereas others were moved by calculations of national interest. This is precisely the point about the failure of attempts to draw straight causal lines from A to B. Members of the Resistance diverged from the Nazis at various stages and they converged with the plot from different starting points and along different lines.

What we often find is that the idea of resistance to Hitler occurred early in the process but was unsystematic and sporadic. Sometimes, the form which it took could lead to an accommodation. Aristocratic nationalists could often coexist with Nazis, even if they despised them. They went part of the way with the Nazis and were compromised. They sympathized with the aim of German greatness and their opposition was weakened. As events developed, the grounds for opposition became clearer and stronger. The strategic situation altered.

In summary, we can conclude that ideological acceleration is not a linear process which produces inevitable outcomes. There are always alternatives and therefore there are always exits.

Movements which succeed generally offer solutions to overwhelming problems as a first inducement to join. They have recruiting practices which apply gentle persuasion, and they create cultures of their own. The processes are not mysterious. What baffles us is the outcome when we have not seen the stages by which it has been produced. "How," we wonder, "did the toothpaste get into the tube?"

In the final section of this chapter I shall look at two leaders, using them as examples of developmental transformation.

Psychobiographies of leaders

Perhaps it would be a good idea to state the purpose of psycho-biography clearly. I do not maintain that childhood conflicts explain ideologies; I do maintain that conflicts from childhood are sometimes continued in an ideological form when an ideology is found which offers a perfect dramatization and intellectu-alizaton of an early struggle. Is there anything mysterious in this? We may say that X developed a passionate hatred of arbitrary authority as a result of childhood experiences, and that this explains at least in part why she searches for a cause and dedi-cates herself to it throughout her life. What seems to be strange to those who are less passionate is the degree of self-sacrifice and also the way in which she reads the same struggle into every situation. She is always against the establishment and always idealizes the oppressed in an unrealistic way, believing their every promise and justification. She splits the world into black and white, into good and bad, in a way that reminds us of child-hood games. Experience appears to have taught her nothing about the mixtures and compromises of the real world. She repeatedly enacts the struggle against authority in the hope that one day authority will disappear. Until then, authority is evil and its opponents are good.

The questions which the psychobiographer often asks are: Why the simplification? Why the intensity? Why the repetition?

From our discussion of ideological acceleration we can see that there is a protracted process of learning during which we assimi-late the story of a world split into insiders and outsiders, into the deserving and the undeserving and, for some special utopian sto-ries, into good and evil. This story represents personal conflict as social conflict; the only novel thing about developmental accounts is that we posit a special readiness to learn the story and a special readiness to believe it and sometimes a special zeal in trying to do something about it. It is the excess that interests us as psychobiographers. The stories themselves are part of our cul-tural heritage and are subject to the normal processes of social modification and institutionalization. Occasionally, the fanatic

111

will play a part in shaping the story. Just as often, his major contribution will be in acting out a widely accepted script.

Two examples of psychobiography will be given to enable us to evaluate the possible contribution of this approach to political behaviour. The subjects of these psychobiographies are Hitler and Stalin.

Adolf Hitler

Hitler has often been used as an example of someone whose personal problems were ideologized and thus invested with the passion required to sustain him through difficult times. Binion (1976), Langer (1972) and Waite (1977) are among those who have supplied us with details of Hitler's Oedipus complex and masochistic sexual perversions. The difficulty is that they tend to take a straight line from childhood trauma to Hitler's quest for *Lebensraum* in Russia and his apparently self-destructive decision to halt the German tanks short of Dunkirk thus allowing the British Expeditionary Force to escape. If the thesis of ideological transformation presented above is correct, unresolved personal conflicts are indeed important; but what is needed is a demonstration of how these personal conflicts are converted into social acts which may resolve them, so that the individual is "ideologically cured". When that happens, ideological struggle is the continuation of neurotic conflict by other means.

Whatever the case, the new struggle at the social level has conditions, gains and losses of its own which must be taken into consideration when explaining events. Recurrent patterns (such as self-destructive behaviour) should be offered as an explanation only after the situational logic of the behaviour has been carefully investigated. Hitler may have halted the tanks short of Dunkirk because he was following von Rundstedt's advice that the tanks had outrun their lines of supply and needed refitting (Cocks,1986). And what was the urgency? Did anyone believe that the British would escape given German control of the air? Goering promised to finish the job and it was rational to believe that he could. Hitler was not short of technical advice on which to act. There are times when hypotheses derived from psycho-biography can be used to explain a leader's decisions but these hypotheses have to be evaluated against competing ones. It is not the case that psychological factors sometimes operate and some-times do not, but rather that each event has a number of causes which have to be looked at. Among these are such factors as what information is available, who is present, how the alterna-tives are presented, whether the leader has already committed himself to a decision, whether there is a consensus which has to be reversed, whether the matter is one which is linked to some previously developed doctrine, whether everyone is excessively fatigued and what the leader's health is like. We know that in the later years of the war Hitler's health was bad and this may have contributed to many bad decisions.

What we shall try to do is to reconstruct Hitler's identity conflict and see to what extent the ideological transformation of this con-flict explains his virulent hatred of Jews. Anyone in Germany might have hated Jews, given the prevalence of anti-semitism, but only for some did it become an obsession. We do not set aside the social explanation — in fact we rely on it to construct the ideological accelerator — and we do not regard the two explanations as mutually exclusive. People start the process of ideological transformation with certain predispositions. These, as well as the influences to which they are subjected, determine what happens. Some of the properties of individuals entering the ideological accelerator are explained by the culture which they share with many others, and the process of ideological accelera-tion works on these cultural elements — values, beliefs and prac-tices; but other properties are the result of idiosyncratic varia-tions in personal history. This provides opportunities for both the psychobiographer, studying particular variations within a culture, and the social psychologist, studying variations between cultures, as long as neither is simple-minded enough to draw a straight line from cause to effect. Process is the important thing to bear in mind — process in which there are many steps. We should not imagine that we can determine the menu by specifying a cow and a vegetable patch. We now return to Hitler..

Though we know a little about Hitler's early life, we do not know enough to answer most of our questions. But this is the way that all interesting scientific enterprises begin (such as paleontology or history).

Hitler's mother gave birth to him after losing three children and we can imagine that there was an anxious intensity in their relationship. At any rate, it was close and protective. His father, who was 23 years older than his mother, had never known his own father (who was said to be a Jew). Is this important? Hitler is said to have made some efforts later on to trace his Jewish ancestor, so the matter may have occupied his mind.

We can understand Hitler's anxiety about "tainted blood" — an anxiety which is expressed again and again in his rage against the Jews and foreign blood — when we recall that, of the children born to the marriage of his parents, four died prematurely, one was hidden as an idiot child and one, his sister Paula, was described by a physician as a high grade moron (Waite, 1971). The near incestuous marriage of his parents (Alois was Klara's uncle and had to get special Papal dispensation for the marriage) added to this anxiety. We may note here that in the great love of his life for his niece Geli Raubal (the only woman he ever really loved according to him) he duplicated the uncle/niece relationship of his mother and father.

Hitler's father was harsh and cruel to his family. He died and was not regretted. But the adolescent Hitler then lost his mother: she died of cancer while being cared for by a Jewish physician who recalled, thirty years later, that he had never in all his career seen anyone as prostrate with grief as Adolf Hitler. Hitler's early life was a series of failures. He failed to get admitted to the Viennese Academy of Fine Arts and blamed Jewish influence for this. He lived in hostels largely supported by Jewish charities. His relations with women remained so full of conflict throughout his life that four of them committed suicide or attempted to do so. He was at his most vigorous during the First World War, becoming a good soldier and winning a decoration. His apathy vanished and he took pride in his service. Then came the defeat of Germany. He was in hospital recovering his sight after a mustard gas attack and he went blind again, possibly psychosomatically. He recovered when his mission became clear. He would go into politics to save Germany from the Jews and Marxists. In describing his recovery he writes in *Mein Kampf* : "There is no making pacts with Jews; there can only be the hard: either — or." He would obey the voice of his conscience and avenge the sufferings of those who had fought for the fatherland.

From that moment on, Hitler had a cause in life. He had the "holy mission" of defending Germany against the Jews who were the enemies within and without, as he wrote in *Mein Kampf*. All the enemies of Germany, all those who had betrayed her and stabbed her in the back and raped her and infected her and plundered her were either "Jews" or "Jew-lovers". Jews could be blamed for almost anything. Speaking to an audience of women in 1934 he said: "The phrase 'Emancipation of Woman' is only an invention of the Jewish intellect and its content is stamped with the same spirit. In the really good periods of German life the German woman never needed to emancipate herself" (Baynes,1942, p. 731).

How could Hitler's inner struggle to save his mother become a war against Jews and how could this become part of the programme of a historically decisive political movement? The crucial move was to discover who had been responsible for his own failures, the death of his mother and the betrayal of Germany. The answer was: the Jews. To understand the emotional power of this conviction, we should realise that it solved several problems for him. It solved the problem of understanding his own failure and relieved him of responsibility for it. It solved the problem of how the generation of soldiers at the front had been betrayed and relieved "Germany" (the old, true and entirely fictitious "Germany") of the responsibility for this betrayal. And, at the deepest developmental level, it relieved him of the impossible burden of failing to protect his mother as he should have. He should have compensated his mother for the failure of her incestuous marriage to a brutal man of Jewish ancestry, to put it most starkly. (The "legend" of Jewish ancestry is the significant thing here: it is what Hitler suspected and feared.) Children frequently have impossible family tasks delegated to them, as Helm Stierlin pointed out in his analysis of Hitler's family. Usually these tasks remain private concerns and lead only to private and personal complications. Occasionally, private problems can be ideologically transformed and politicized. Such a politicization would not have been possible but for the circumstances of Germany between the wars. It would not have been possible if the culture and ideology of anti-semitism had not already been in place among the various strands of German culture.

When the *Protocols of the Learned Elders of Zion* with its details of the "Jewish conspiracy against the Christians" appeared in German translation in 1920, it became a best seller. By the end of the year, 120,000 copies had been sold. (The *Protocols* are still a best seller: Kedourie (1992) tells us that in Algeria the Front Islamique du Salut denounces "Liberty, equality, fraternity" as slogans spread by the *Protocols* to corrupt the world and calls for the re-establishment of the Caliphate over the whole Muslim world.)

What was needed was a cowardly and cunning enemy to solve the problem of how Germany could have been defeated and how it could continue to be humiliated by its enemies. The Jews fitted the bill. There had been a conspiracy. Many Germans believed what Hitler was prepared to say. Hitler needed a vile enemy to explain both his own situation as a talented man who had been thwarted in his ambitions and his position as a German who had seen Germany cheated out of its dominant position in Europe. An old manner of speaking is often used to give utterance to a current emotion. Since the Jews are the image of all that is treacherous, hatred of the Jews can be used to express our feeling of betrayal. The primitive logic of hatred would run: "You can see how much we hate you by the way we express our hatred of the Jews. And you will see by the way we treat them how dangerous and implacable we are to our enemies. For the moment we cannot do anything to you, but wait!"

Hitler dramatized the emotions which so many felt. Some were with him all the way and believed his theories. Some had personal identity problems which energized their theories of history. Others sipped the pleasure of anti-semitism in passing conversations, in sneering jokes, in cutting remarks, or in their own imaginations. Hitler was not different from the others. He merely had, or so the psychobiographer would argue, a more highly charged obsession than most and a greater capacity to

116

implement his obsession. Many report the effect of his speeches on them. Albert Speer, in his autobiography, describes how he walked in a trance after listening to Hitler speak to students at the university. Leni Riefenstahl describes in her autobiography how she first saw and heard Hitler at the Berlin Sportpalast in 1932. When she heard him begin "Fellow Germans!" she had "an almost apocalyptic vision" that she was never able to forget. She later produced her film, "Triumph of the Will" about the Nazi party rally in Nuremberg in 1934 which shows Hitler descending to crowds who are in a state of mass hysteria. In it she celebrates the power and passion of the spectacle.

The power and the passion derive from the shared emotions of the crowd. They had not come to celebrate the resolution of Hitler's private identity crisis, but the resolution of a crisis common to all: the crisis of failure. They watched Hitler begin his speeches, nervous and tentative, like Germany herself in the catastrophes of 1918 and 1929. They watched him become the pitiless and all-powerful Leader who would save Germany, save them all. What effect might Hitler's speeches have had on someone like Herr Neisse, Christabel Bielenberg's gardener who was described near the beginning of the preceding chapter? We have little difficulty in recognizing him as someone who wanted to believe in Germany's greatness (and his own security). He wanted a powerful Germany to protect him against the storm and wrack of change. He could not lead. Hitler offered him a romantically touched up picture of a Germany which had never existed but one which ought to have existed for all true patriots. It would be purified so that it would be better than ever. Once the purification was complete, Herr Neisse would be able to take up the position to which he was entitled — one of respect. To watch a performance by Hitler was to take part in a dramatic restoration of part of Germany's culture, the culture of the*Machtstaat* inaugurated under Bismarck.

Hitler told Germans that they had been weakened by their very virtues, by the virtues that made them most German. That had been the diabolical cunning of the Jew. Germans would be forced to become less German for a while in order to prevail. This was the spectacle which he presented to the fascinated gaze of Germany. It had been a theme from the beginning. In an interview in July 1933 he said:

"Am I to allow thousands of pure-blooded Germans to perish so that all Jews may work, live and be merry in security while a nation of millions is a prey to starvation, despair and bolshevism?" (Baynes,1942, p. 729).

Indeed not. But it required someone as diabolical as Hitler to demonize the Jews to the point where their genocide seemed like patriotism.

Iosif Djugashvili (Stalin)

Let us start with some of the characteristics of the adult Stalin and then see if we can understand how they developed and how they influenced the Soviet state.

Bukharin states what many historians now believe — that the mainspring of Stalin's personality was the need to triumph vindictively over his enemies, and since he thought of all who surpassed him as enemies, there were many to conquer (Tucker, 1973, p. 424).

He had to beat people, and this meant both physically beat them and overcome them. Towards the end of his life, judges interrogating a group of doctors charged with conspiring to shorten the lives of Soviet leaders were instructed to "Beat, beat, and, once again, beat" (Ibid. p. 74). This predisposition of Stalin's combined well with a revolutionary culture which emphasized terror and an "exemplary lack of mercy" (Lenin). "It would be the greatest mistake to think that the New Economic Policy has put an end to terror. We will return to terror and economic terror" (Lenin, cited in Volkogonov 1991, p. 559). The language preferred by both bolsheviks and Stalin was to "overthrow", "destroy", "crush", "break", "unmask", and "nail down". The conspiratorial party met the perfect conspirator: Stalin. The Party's attempts to turn away from state terror were left too long. The mistake was to believe that what had been appropriate for revolutionary activity would also be appropriate for the conduct of government.

Stalin believed that authority should inspire fear, especially among the top officials of the state. With the exception of Beria, the chief instrument of his terror, who often drove to Stalin's villa with Malenkov, they were never allowed to assemble in groups of two or more without his permission (Volkoganov, 1991).

In a study entitled "Political Culture and Leadership" (1987), Tucker summarizes Stalin's core as follows: Stalin had a neurotic and compulsive need to prove that he was Lenin's equal; and to do this he had to match Lenin's revolutionary success of October 1917. Stalin's attempt at "revolution from above" — the forced industrialization of Russia in the 1930s — was his attempt to show that he was as great as Lenin. He failed and repressed knowledge of that failure, yet at the same time he could not avoid suspecting that others were aware of it. This led to an insatiable need to extract flattery and to punish others for their unspoken criticisms or "deviations". Hence the forced confessions of unspoken and mysterious crimes. The real crime, the one which no one could admit because it was never mentioned, was that the criminals did not think even more highly of Stalin than he did himself.

Can we explain any of this, firstly by looking at Stalin's own development and secondly at the culture of the movement?

Stalin's childhood was in some respects a replica of Hitler's. He had a violent and drunken father whom he hated and despised and a mother who was devoted to him. She had also buried three children before she had Stalin. It was said that "he was devoted to one person — his mother". She invested her aspirations in him and idolized him. Unfortunately, to become an idol is a very bad preparation for the real world. One is unlikely to be worshipped in the manner to which one has become accustomed. So what is the answer? For most people of course it is to give up being an idol, but in very rare and bloody cases one may insist on one's destiny. That is what Stalin did. He was a rebel in childhood; he was a rebel when he studied in the seminary to be a priest; and he became a revolutionary. But always he believed that he was right and that he was destined for greatness. In his formative years he identified with Koba, a character in a popular Georgian novel, who fought both against the Russians and against the Georgian nobles who supported them for the favours they could gain. Koba fought for the people. This identification with Koba was taken so seriously that he took it as his first revolutionary name.

How could this Georgian identify with Russia and surrender Georgian nationalism? He joined Russia by joining the bolsheviks, as Tucker says in his biography. There had been two strands in his earlier identification with Koba. The first had been the attack on the Tsarist government. The second had been the class war of the poor against the rich and the nobility. Bolshevism emphasized the second and suppressed the first. Koba also had difficulties with the Georgians. They did not appreciate him. It was clear that the shift from Georgia to Russia was a shift to the winning side. "Lenin made the transition to Russian identity all the easier for Djugashvili by virtue of his anger against official Russia and everything associated with it" (Tucker, 1973, p. 143). He could still hate Russia. He could also love it. The time had come to change from Koba to Stalin.

The revolutionary culture to which Stalin responded was conspiratorial and ruthless. The bolsheviks had chosen a conspiratorial route against the Mensheviks. They had chosen to overturn the elections to the Constituent Assembly of 1917, elections in which they had obtained less than a quarter of the representatives and to instal the dictatorship of the proletariat. They had been compelled to fight a vicious war to remain in power. The point is that they had chosen to instal a government which would act as though it was a means of perpetuating the revolution. This is the weapon that Stalin took from Lenin and wielded with ever greater ferocity. The tradition of "revolution from above" had been practised by the Tsars, by Ivan the Terrible and by Peter the Great. Stalin approved. Who else could do what had to be done? Who else would want to?

The strategy in this account of Stalin is to see him as a person peculiarly fitted to exploit a revolutionary culture. This fitness is the result of a process of socialization which began in childhood and continued in the movement. He was particularly well prepared by earlier rebellion to identify with the struggle and by the experience of violence to identify with revolutionary methods. His mother's idolization of him made him ambitious to occupy the pinnacle and impatient of any gods beside himself. But he had not been immaculately conceived, nor had others immediately recognized that he was entitled to the admiration he claimed. They had criticized; some had tried to get the better of him. In the party, he had not been thought of as the natural heir of Lenin. He would have to show them. And he would have to show the millions who stood in the way of his plans that he was not to be resisted.

Stalin developed a perfect psychological trick for dealing with enemies. He divided the world into hostile camps: those who were in the Party and those who were not. The moment anyone attacked or even criticized him, he construed that person as being anti-party. This meant that any criticism of him (by someone who was by definition anti-Party) merely confirmed his own ideal position as being the enemy of all enemies of the Party. So he suffered and took his revenge.

Concluding comments

A psychology of genocide should give first place to culture and its institutional contexts. All movements make use of existing cultures and then transform them. This is the burden of the accounts of ideological transformation and acceleration in this chapter. And all movements have to be led. This is why we have paid particular attention to the psychobiographies of leaders.

The final chapter of this book is about the future of genocide. Can we find ways of preventing it?

CHAPTER EIGHT

THE FUTURE OF GENOCIDE

It would be a very happy ending if we could now forecast the end of genocide and say that we have good strategies for stopping it wherever it occurs. Our failure in Bosnia shows how false this is. The political problems of intervention are as formidable as ever. And the fact that there have been over 40 genocidal events since World War II shows that genocide is not rare.

In Chapter 1, I referred to the puzzle of genocide, and described that puzzle as the fact that it often appears to be irrational, in the sense that it does not serve the best interests of those who perpetrate it. At other times, we can see the economic advantage, but it is not consistently sought. I contrasted genocides of colonization, which seem to have clear political and economic advantages, with the Nazi genocide of Jews, gypsies, Slavs, and homosexuals, which was very costly and did not have any clear advantages. Have we come any closer to an answer to these puzzles? I think we have, but our conclusions should now be spelt out.

Irrational genocide is the result of two processes. The first is the process by which rage is redistributed and the second is the competition among political movements. Let us examine the redistribution of hatred first and the social ecology of movements thereafter.

Redistribution of Rage

Political parties exist not only to redistribute goods, but to redistribute rage, anger and hatred. Those who have been filled with rage because of defeat, catastrophe, and frustrated expectations, can either hate themselves or someone else. When we referred to genocidal activators we were pointing to social conditions which gave rise to hatred and fear. By ideological work these private emotions are transformed into collective rage and hatred. This politicization of the private I called ideological transformation. Ideological acceleration completes the separation of the good from the bad and prepares the perpetrators for action against their victims. What we get is a utopia based on terror. There is no compromise between hell and heaven, salvation or damnation, belonging or not belonging. Because the separation is absolute, any step in the wrong direction may have the direst consequences. The external sign of this process of separation is the dehumanization of the victims by foul language, thus preparing them for physical abuse.

Now we are in a position to understand many of the characteristic ideologies of the twentieth century. They are chiefly about the redistribution of hatred. Fascism, Nazism, nationalism, communism, and religious fundamentalism are about the punishment of those who are to blame. They are about smiting the sinners. Of course, the elect are promised good things, but the engine of ideology is hatred. This is why good things for the elect have to be obtained by so much killing. This is why the struggle for peace has to continue until no house is left standing. All political movements have some anger to redistribute; but under favourable conditions this anger is converted into mere collective dislike or antipathy and can be kept under control. It is subordinated to a rational calculation of interests and we can trust such a movement not to do much more harm than is absolutely necessary. Such a movement is defined primarily by what it is for, rather than by what it is against. It is "rational" and this rationality is the basis of stable government. Deals can be struck, compromises can be arranged, and black shades into white through a dozen different greys. Parties which have to redistribute hatred create unstable governments because they are so busy making enemies and separating the population into those who are for them and those who are against them that they become involved in fruitless wars as well as genocidal massacres.

It is significant that so much of the politics before us in the declining years of the century is the politics of rage and hatred. Why should this be so?

Firstly, many liberation movements are not concerned with liberty. When empires fell (the Ottoman, the European, the Soviet) the liberation movements were defined, as often as not, by what they were opposed to rather than what they were for; what they were in fact for was often simply power for an elite, though they promised liberty. As a consequence, many people have been disappointed. They have become poorer, and they are threatened by intolerant movements which had been restrained under empire. If we had understood the ecology of culture better, we would have predicted this. When empires fall, struggles for domination start all over again, often driven by ideologies which functioned well in the struggle against authority, but which do badly in the attempt to establish tolerant government. Nationalist ideologies (in all their guises), mobilize people to rebel, but often become instruments of tyranny in multicultural states. They have been shaped by hatred during the years of struggle and this hatred usually remains the core of the movement after the old regime has been overthrown; but now it is redirected against former allies, other ethnic groups, and rival movements. The point here should be abundantly clear by now. Most modern states are irreversibly multicultural and one of the criteria by which we should judge a political movement is the degree to which it recognizes this and takes active steps to enable cultural diversity to flourish. Many of the liberation movements which have been so much admired fail this test dismally. They are a disaster to most of the people in their countries. What they redistribute is rage and hatred, not goods.

We should identify and study the role of keystone authorities in preserving multicultural society, defining a keystone authority as one which has an interest in cultural diversity. When it is removed, multicultural society decays into a less diverse condition. Here I have borrowed Robert Paine's concept of keystone species from ecology, where a keystone species is one which preserves diversity. Starfish play this role in intertidal communities of limpets, chitons, barnacles, whelks, brachiopods and other invertebrates. If the starfish is removed, the community collapses and diversity is reduced (Terborgh, 1992). Each society contains different cultural movements which are hostile to each other and are only kept from destroying each other by keystone authorities. After the French Revolution of 1789, to cite an example, the cultural diversity of France was reduced by a deliberate campaign against regional languages and cultures. To summarize, the collapse of keystone authorities frequently brings the rise of predatory political movements dedicated to a reduction in cultural diversity and to a redistribution of hatred rather than the creation of new goods.

This leads straight on to the second reason why the politics of rage will continue: intractable poverty.

Attempts to deal with Third World poverty have not been particularly successful. Aid has been based on the simple assumption that if you lend or give people assistance it will be good for them. We have by now seen that this is false. Aid can be beneficial only where it is carefully adjusted to the capacity of the receiving country to use it. In some cases, it is like extending credit to a drunken lout. Aid can increase dependency, ruin local farmers by flooding countries with free food, strengthen local racketeers who control distribution, increase corruption, and strengthen despotic governments.

Poverty is with us to stay. In the USA, the gap between the poor and the rich shows no signs of narrowing. More significantly, the gap between poor and rich countries shows no signs of narrowing. Some countries are now sustained permanently by aid — Bangladesh, Haiti, El Salvador, Somalia — and there are no signs of an improvement in the situation. The major problem is population increase (compounded by political disorder and poor policies). The worst is Bangladesh, with a population of 774 people per square kilometre, or 0.08 hectares of cropland per person. And the population is still increasing at a spectacular rate. Overall, world population is increasing at a rate of 1.7 percent per annum and the production of cereals at 0.9 percent. This growing food deficit is expected to cause the number of food-related deaths to increase from 200 million in the last twenty years to 1,000 million in the next twenty (Perutz,1992). When we talk of a global population increase of 90 million per year, we are talking of an increase which approximates to the total population of a state such as Germany; and to make things worse, the greatest increase in population is in the poorest countries. Other figures, whether of energy consumption, production, or trade, show the same picture of a widening gap. The point here is that there is a lot of misery waiting to be converted into anger and directed at enemies. These need not necessarily be the richest nations. Hatred may be directed against hostage groups or neighbours who appear to have blighted the hopes of the people. Violence is usually directed at first against the weakest targets. In revolutionary situations, members of the oppressed first attack each other. To shape a revolutionary movement it is often necessary to kill many more members of the constituency it purports to represent (so-called collaborators), than of the ostensible enemy. Movements are produced by terror directed as much against their "spontaneous" supporters as against their enemies. This was the experience of anti-colonial movements in Algeria, India and Indo-China. It is also the experience in South Africa where black on black violence far exceeds black on white violence.

Yet we should not underestimate the potential for rage and hatred directed against rich countries by the poor countries, often with the greatest justification. What is lacking is not so much motive as opportunity for the expression of this hatred. And there are ideologues who would like to channelize it. Gaddafi has made attempts, by expounding a Third Theory (cribbed from the Algerian writer Malek Bennabi), according to which the true division of the world is not between East and West or communism and capitalism, but between North and South (Kedourie, 1980, p. 63). According to this theory, the Moslem world is the centre of gravity of the underdeveloped countries of the South and will direct their struggle against the North. There is an outward direction — against the North — and there is an inward direction, which is the creation of an Islamic utopia. The crucial question, as Kedourie observes, is the effect of a utopian blueprint which has almost no contact with realities on the conduct of politics. He concludes that, for utopians:

> Political discourse ceases to be a way of dealing with emergencies in a customary and familiar manner, and becomes a series of logical-seeming imperatives to which all citizens must, at all costs, be committed (Ibid. p. 64).

The fact that a discourse is of little value for creating goods does not mean that it is not extremely useful in the redistribution of hatred. There is often an inverse relationship. The more the discourse fails to support the normal production of goods, the more it is used to show who is responsible for this failure.

The volatile relationship between the rich and the poor may be illustrated with an example from the recent Gulf war. What is significant is the way in which support for Saddam developed even among those who had an interest in opposing him, such as Pakistanis. Pakistan had good reason to oppose Saddam's invasion of Kuwait and to support the USA since over 60,000 Pakistanis work in Kuwait contributing 40% of remittances from abroad to Pakistan and there are many economic and political ties between the USA and Pakistan. When the invasion occurred there was much sympathy for Kuwait, and Pakistan committed 10,000 troops to the UN alliance against Saddam. Yet the moment the bombing started, the popular mood changed. Bush and Major were tried and burnt in effigy in the marketplaces. It was argued that Iraq had been lured into attacking Kuwait so that it could be destroyed by the diabolical West. Saddam was portrayed by the media as a hero of Islam. He was the champion of the poor against the corruption of the Kuwaiti ruling family; he supported the PLO; he called for a Jihad (Ahmed, 1991). The hideous sight of unresisted air strikes so triumphantly shown on television revived images of European attacks on helpless Third World peoples.

What was the effect of this? Saddam became suddenly popular throughout the Muslim world and even among the non-Muslim poor. The Supreme Council of British Muslims met in Bradford and unanimously supported Saddam's invasion of Kuwait — and this in spite of the fact that Kuwait is a major donor to many Muslim organizations in Britain. What on earth could have moved British Muslims to support a thug like Saddam? A simple analogy: Saddam is to the USA (the UN was seen as a mere instrument of the West) as British Muslims are to the British. The media played their role by constantly portraying Saddam as a Muslim and a weirdo and linking him with Arafat, Gaddafi and Khomeini. They gloried in the overwhelming might of the West with its vast technological sophistication. What became important to the underdogs was that Saddam had challenged the West and was now at the receiving end. He fought for Islam against the West and against Israel. What mattered in the thick of the fray was heroic resistance, being with one's own people, being of the faith, and attacking those who had humiliated the poor of the world.

There is no reason to expect that things will improve in the short or even the long run unless there are radical new directions in policy. At the moment it is difficult to see what they could be. Nor should the rich nations feel secure because of their overwhelming technological superiority. The poor have less to lose, they are angrier, and the limits of revolutionary blackmail and terror have been imagined but not yet seen. The essence of victory in armed struggle is that it goes to the side which first convinces its opponent that it can inflict intolerable punishment. This is not necessarily the greater punishment nor is it always inflicted by the side which has the most resources. The barbarian cycle described by the classical Arab historian Ibn Kaldun over five centuries ago is still an important factor: as life gets better and better for the rich, they become less and less inclined to sacrifice themselves to preserve it, whereas those with nothing become more and more available for ideologies which inspire revenge. The rage which produces genocidal and other violent movements is continually being generated and intervention to deal with it will often cost more than the rich are prepared to contemplate. This was true in the past, it is true in the present (apparently nothing can be done about either Bosnia or East Timor) and it is likely to be true of the future.

So far we have discussed the first factor in irrational genocide: it is the result of attempts to redistribute hatred. It is the politics of rage and can only be understood as such.

But there is another factor in producing irrational outcomes: they are built into the process of conflict. Freud told a story to account for the apparently crazy decisions which people take. If we drop the notion that the person is a single, undivided being and accept that persons are divided internally into warring parts, then many of the results make more sense. He cited the couple who are given three wishes. The husband is terribly hungry and wishes for a sausage. This waste of a wish makes his wife so angry that she wishes the sausage would stick to his nose. What can they do now? If they are well disposed towards each other they can wish that everything would return to the state it was in before. If they are still in conflict, terrible things can happen — irrational things! Similarly, since "society" is not a single, undivided entity, the outcome of conflict between different parts of it will often seem irrational. The outcome is often what no one wants. Let us explain all of this more fully by looking at the social ecology of political movements.

Social Ecology

Political movements compete in environments which sometimes favour one kind of movement and sometimes another (so that we could describe one kind of environment as consisting of genocide activators); political movements vary enormously in their character (so that some could be decribed as genocidal, others as merely violent and yet others as pacifist); some solutions to the interaction between movements and their environments occur fairly frequently (so that we can classify genocide scenarios). Now what I shall attempt to do is to set all this out in a fairly formal way so that we can see the implications of this ecological approach as clearly as possible.

Social Ecology of Genocidal Movements

Fundamental Assumption

In every society there is a range of movements from genocidal to pacifist. They compete with each other for political power.

Corollaries

1.   The fate of every movement depends on what all the other movements do.
   [This means that they devise strategies to compete and the success or failure of those strategies depends on what others

are doing, not how "good" or "bad" the strategies are in isolation.]

2.   Since each movement has a limited time in which to adapt, the outcome is always imperfect and is usually botched.
        [Things are not for the best in this best of possible worlds. Neither are they for the worst.]

3.   Perfection is further limited by the fact that each movement starts with its own ideas and tools, many of which are frankly absurd and inefficient.
        [What happens depends in part on where we start from.]

4.   The fate of every movement depends also on variations in the environment.
        [As we have seen, bad times and power vacuums favour violent movements. We also have to allow for chance and luck. Your strategy may be excellent but luck may be against you because you have rotten cards.]

5.   The spread of ideological elements depends on their packaging in an ideology.
        [An ideology is a set of elements called "ideologemes". The ideologeme of "dictatorship of the proletariat" rides as part of the liberation ideology of Marxism and it may spread, not because people want dictatorship in any form, but because they want liberation. Given the choice between liberation and supporting the old regime they choose liberation — and take dictatorship on board.
        Another example: many people in Germany supported the Nazi ideology for its promise of folkish community, national honour, full employment, and getting rid of the old hierarchical social structure and colluded in genocide at a much later stage.
        The point about "packaging" is that it produces some extraordinary effects. An ideologeme may spread widely without being central to the popularity of a movement; yet it may have devastating effects and be more noticeable retrospectively than any other characteristics of the movement. Lewontin's (1990) observations of genetic hitch-hiking inspired this observation.
        Finally, people may acquiesce in what a movement does because its ideas can be attached to existing ideas. This "host

susceptibility" paralyzes resistance. In Nazi Germany, many who were not genocidal were nevertheless anti-semitic. This weakened resistance.]

6.   Movements exist in communities of different degrees of cultural variety.

[Some communities are relatively heterogeneous because of historical mingling and conquests. This variety is maintained or reduced by keystone authorities. Some, typically nationalist movements, attempt to reduce cultural variety; others, such as imperial powers, attempt to preserve variation or at least live with it as part of the idea of empire.]

The consequences of this approach to the social ecology of political movements are fundamental. They are:

*History is unpredictable.
*The "best" can expect to triumph only under special
  circumstances, and certainly only if they work very
  hard at their strategic planning.
*Those movements which do triumph are not
  necessarily optimally adapted to circumstances.
  They can be outwitted.
*Terrible movements, including genocidal movements,
  will keep emerging.

Directions

How can we reduce the number of genocides? We should attempt to move on four broad fronts:
  *Deepen our understanding of the social ecology of
    genocide.
  *Establish the right to intervene and the capacity to
    intervene.
  *Learn to unpack ideologies.
  *Prepare ourselves psychologically to recognize and
    resist genocidal temptations.

Let us look at these approaches one by one.

Understanding Social Ecology

Here we have provided a justification of the ecological approach, already implicit in many formulations of policy, such as the Marshall Aid programme to assist European recovery after World War II. The argument there was clearly an ecological argument: make Europe prosperous and totalitarian movements will not flourish. This sounds simple, yet it only works if aid is given in the right way to countries with the expertise and political structures to receive it. Aid is of little value if it is used to enrich political leaders and is not used to build up the productive capacity and independence of the recipient. Making the environment unsuitable for genocidal movements is clearly a difficult job which will require much further study.

Right and capacity to intervene

Intervention to prevent genocide has occurred in the past, but it will only become effective with practice. We see in Bosnia how difficult and ineffective it is to police genocide with the present UN resources.

The right to intervene on behalf of persecuted nations has long been part of the law of nations (Kuper,1985). In 1827 England, France and Russia intervened in the Graeco-Turkish war to stop atrocities. In 1840 the USA intervened with the Sultan of Turkey to end the persecution of the Jews of Damascus and Rhodes. In 1861 France intervened in the Lebanon. In 1902 the USA directed a remonstrance to the government of Romania to end its persecution of Jews. In 1915 France, Great Britain and Russia protested against the massacre of Armenians in Turkey. More recently, the UN has been the instrument of a number of peace missions. But these are not successful unless backed by a major power for its own reasons, often to such an extent that the UN action is seen as a Great Power action in disguise. The history of the interventions listed above is not impressive; but at least the right has been established and some advances made towards creating international political machinery for carrying them out. None of this removes or solves any of the strategic questions about intervention. Does a particular intervention do more good than harm?   What, for example, will the balance be in the Gulf?   On the one hand, 200,000 dead, the continued tyranny of Saddam and the persecution of Kurds and Shi'ites; on the other the containment of the military adventures of a dangerous dictator and the "liberation" of Kuwait.

The right to bring war criminals, torturers, and genocides to trial has also been established and this may in time be a significant move. If it can be established in international law that persons who have been engaged in crimes against humanity can be apprehended for those crimes wherever they are found and put on trial before an internationally recognized court, this might act as a deterrent, particularly if the names and faces of wanted suspects are widely publicized in advance through the media. Yet the difficulties are great. Many criminals become political leaders and are regarded as indispensable for the success of negotiations to establish new regimes. Pol Pot is one example.

Ideological unpacking

We should be educated to analyze ideologies and unpack them. Unpacking can only be useful if the person doing the unpacking has standards and convictions to resist dangerous ideologies. Nihilists may find ideological baubles, no matter how poisonous, fascinating; and it is possible that nihilist attitudes favoured the spread of the politics of rage in Europe in the earlier part of the century. But what do we mean by nihilism?   It is the attitude that lies are as good as the truth, that a convenient lie is certainly better than an inconvenient truth, if such a thing as truth exists, and that truths are merely the lies of those in power.   Goering expressed his nihilist vision with his usual skill: "I am proud of not knowing what justice is" (von Schlabrendorff, 1965, p. 55). With widespread nihilism, a small group of fanatics can easily take over. We have already cited some evidence to show that at the start of the Hitler period most Germans were politically apathetic and that only a small number were either actively pro-Nazi or anti-Nazi. Their indifference (this is von Schlabrendorff's thesis) made it impossible to rally them to resist after Hitler had been legally installed as Chancellor. There were no moral values strong enough to counter their respect for legally constituted authority, no matter how immoral it was. In fact, even members of the Catholic Centre Party were attempting to do deals with Hitler. And many were delighted to have Hitler in the government so that he could be tamed. "When Breitscheid heard that Hitler had been appointed Chancellor he clapped his hands together in delight, exclaiming that now Hitler would soon be finished because he would never be able to cope with the difficulties of the Government!" (von Schlabrendorff, 1965, pp. 23-24). Any amount of unpacking will be useless if people do not have a moral resistance to what they unpack. They see the poison, but decide that there's nothing to be done except swallow it.

Psychological preparation

We should learn to recognize lies and violence; but since both are the very life of politics and much of what passes for education, there are some difficulties in this proposal. Let me spell it out. When adolescents are taught about any injustice done to their group (however this may be interpreted in various cultures), they should simultaneously learn about an injustice their own group has done to others. In South Africa (to take an example close to me), when white Afrikaners were taught in school about the wrongs done to them by the British, they should simultaneously have been taught about the wrongs they were doing to Blacks. Comparisons should be deliberate and unsparing. What we want is not the posturing of the victim or the perpetrator; we must encourage the integrity and understanding of the fallible but loving human soul. We must make reciprocity the intellectual and moral foundation of our education for thinking and acting on social issues. "How do things look from the perspectives of other people?" must become the automatic question when we look at social problems.

There is a very real danger of nihilism if we pursue this kind of education in the wrong way. We have already argued that unpacking lies is no good if we are not able to resist them. What we need, therefore, is a strong commitment to the well-being of all humankind and of the whole planet. Multiculturalism is the social equivalent of polyspeciesism. It is searching for arrangements which enable diversity to flourish to whatever extent is possible. It is, in fact, the exact opposite of the attitudes of the nihilist.

Nihilists do not respect any truth because they do not believe in truth; pluralists respect different truths because they believe in a variety of perspectives and in a variety of worlds each with its own integrity. In fact, that's why they value them. They know that all rich cultures are open to the influence of other cultures and that they have borrowed many ideas, artefacts and practices. Religions, foodstuffs, theories, instruments have passed from culture to culture. Without a variety of cultures we will reduce the interest and value of our lives. This is the aesthetic argument. The utilitarian argument is equally cogent, if not more so. Different cultures are sources of ideas, attitudes and artefacts which we may need to survive the crises of the future. Only monocultural idiots can believe that their own cultures have all the answers. Cultural variety is important for almost exactly the same reasons as biological variety.

But where's the idealism? Perhaps the interest and fascination of understanding the world from several perspectives will keep us occupied, and idealism will be found in fighting for the survival of the planet rather than the survival of the tribe or even the human species.

It is possible. One sees an awakening interest in life — all life — that may yet enable us to move beyond genocide.

BIBLIOGRAPHY

Abel, T. (1938) *Why Hitler Came into Power: an answer based on the original life stories of six hundred of his followers.* Columbia: New York.

Ahmed, A.S. (1991) The next test for British Muslims; loyalties and leadership in a confused community. *Times Literary Supplement,* February 15, p. 8.

Arendt, H. (1963) *Eichmann in Jerusalem; a report on the banality of evil.* The Viking Press: New York.

Baynes, N.H. (ed.) (1942) *The Speeches of Adolf Hitler, April 1922 - August 1939.* Oxford University Press: Oxford.

Bell, D. (1991) After the age of sinfulness: Lukacs and the mystical roots of revolution. *Times Literary Supplement,* July 26, pp. 5 - 8.

Bielenberg, C. (1984) *The Past is Myself.* London: Corgi.

Binion, R. (1976) *Hitler Among the Germans.* Elsevier: New York.

Bloch, Eduard (1941) *Colliers's Magazine,* March 15, p. 36.

Broszat, M. (1986) The Third Reich and the German people, *in* Bull, H. (ed.) *The Challenge of the Third Reich: the Adam von Trott Memorial Lectures.* Clarendon Press: Oxford, pp. 77 - 94.

Browning, C. (1992) *Ordinary Men: Reserve Police Battalion 101 and the Final Solution in Poland.* HarperCollins: New York.

Bull, H. (1986) *The Challenge of the Third Reich: the Adam von Trott Memorial Lectures.* Clarendon Press: Oxford.

Burgler, R.A. (1990) *The Eyes of the Pineapple: Revolutionary intellectuals and terror in Democratic Kampuchea.* Breitenbach: Saarbrucken and Fort Lauderdale.

Carey, P. (1990) In the shadow of the Angkar. *Times Literary Supplement,* Nov 2 - 8, p. 1172.

Carrier, J-B. cited *in* Weber, E. (1988).

Chalk, F. (1989) Definitions of genocide and their implications for prediction and intervention. *Holocaust and Genocide Studies,* **4,** 149 - 60.

Chalk, F. and Jonassohn, K. (1990) *The History and Sociology of Genocide: analyses and case studies.* Yale University Press: New Haven.

Chandler, D.P. (1983) *A History of Cambodia.* Westview Press: Boulder.

Cocks, G. (1986) Contributions of psychohistory to understanding politics. *In* M.G. Hermann (ed.) *Political Psychology.* Jossey-Bass: San Francisco.

Cohn, N. (1967) *Warrant for Genocide.* Harper and Row: New York.

Conquest, R. (1986) *The Harvest of Sorrow: Soviet collectivization and the terror-famine.* Oxford University Press: New York.

Deak, I. (1992) Strategies of hell. *New York Review of Books.* April 25, pp. 8 -13.

De St Jorre, J. (1972) *The Nigerian Civil War.* Hodder and Stoughton: London.

Deutscher, I. and Deutscher, T. (1984) *The Great Purges.* Basil Blackwell: Oxford and New York.

Drechsler, H. (1980) *"Let Us Die Fighting": the struggle of the Herero and the Nama against German imperialism.* Zed: London.

Du Preez, P. (1980) *The Politics of Identity.* Blackwell: Oxford

Evans, R.J. (1992) Playing for the devil; how much did Furtwängler really resist the Nazis? *Times Literary Supplement,* November 13, pp. 3 - 4.

Fein, H. (1984) Scenarios of genocide: models of genocide and critical responses. *In* I.W. Charney (ed.) *Toward the Understanding and Prevention of Genocide.* Westview Press: Boulder.

Forsyth, F. (1969) *The Biafra Story.* Penguin: Harmondsworth.

Fraser, A. (1992) *The Gypsies.* Blackwell: Oxford.

Furtwängler. Cited *in* Evans, R.J. (1992).

Galeano, E. (1989) *Memory of fire,* 3 vols. Quartet: London.

Ginzburg, E. (1989) *Into the Whirlwind.* Collins Harvill: London.

Gross, W. (1938) National socialist racial thought. In *Germany Speaks; by 21 leading members of party and state.* Thornton Butterworth: London.

Harff, B. and Gurr, T.R. (1988) Toward empirical theory of genocides and politicides: identification and measurement of cases since 1945. *International Studies Quarterly,* **32,** pp. 359 - 71.

Hilberg, R. (1985) *The Destruction of the European Jews,* 3 vols. Holmes and Meier: New York and London.

Hirst, D. (1992) The Islamic holy terror spawned in the slums of Cairo. *The Guardian Weekly,* July 31 - August 6.

Hitler, A. *In* Baynes (1942).

Hitler, A. (1939) *Mein Kampf.* Hurst and Blackett: London.

Hoffmann, P. (1970) *The History of the German Resistance 1933 - 1945.*

Hovanissian, R.G. (ed.) (1986) *The Armenian Genocide in Perspective.* Transaction Publishers: New Brunswick, NJ.

Kedourie, E. (1992) The wretched of Algeria. *Times Literary Supplement,* July 10, pp. 3 - 4.

Kedourie, E. (1980) *Islam in the Modern world.* Mansell: London.

Kelso, C. (1992) The inconvenient nomads deep inside the deep. *The Weekly Mail,* July 24 - 30, p. 12.

Kenrick, D. and Puxon, G. (1972) *The Destiny of Europe's Gypsies.* Sussex University Press: London.

Kettenacker, L. (1985) Social and psychological aspects of the Führer's rule. *In* Koch, H.W. (ed.) *Aspects of the Third Reich.* Macmillan: London pp. 96 - 132.

Kiernan, B. (1985) *How Pol Pot Came to Power; a history of communism in Kampuchea.* Verso: London.

Klee, E. Dressen,W. and Riess,V. (eds) (1992) *"The Good Old Days" : The Holocaust as seen by its perpetators and bystanders.* Free Press: New York.

Kuper, L. (1981) *Genocide.* Yale University Press: New Haven and London.

Kuper, L. (1985) *The Prevention of Genocide.* Yale University Press: New Haven and London.

Langer, W. (1972) *The Mind of Adolf Hitler: the secret service report.* Basic Books: New York.

Lenin. *In* Volkogonoff (1991).

Lewis, B. (1961) *The Emergence of Modern Turkey.* Oxford: Oxford University Press.

Lewontin, R.C. (1990) Fallen angels *New York Review of Books,* June 14, pp. 3 - 7.

Lifton, R.J. (1986) *The Nazi Doctors: medical killing and the psychology of genocide.* Basic Books: New York

Littell, F.H. (1988) Essay: early warning. *Holocaust and Genocide Studies,* **3**, pp. 483 - 90.

Ludlow, P. (1986) Britain and the Third Reich. *In* Bull, H. (ed.) *The Challenge of the Third Reich: the Adam von Trott Memorial Lectures.* Clarendon Press: Oxford pp. 141 - 62.

Mace, J.E. (1988) The politics of famine: American government and press response to the Ukrainian famine, 1932 - 1933. *Holocaust and Genocide Studies,* **3**, pp. 75 - 94.

Mandelstam, N. Cited *in* Bell, D (1991).

Martins-Heuss, K. (1989). Reflections on the collective identity of German Roman and Sinti (Gypsies) after National Socialism. *Holocaust and Genocide Studies,* **4**, pp. 193 - 211.

Mason, T. (1986) The Third Reich and the German left: persecution and resistance. *In* Bull, H. (ed.) *The Challenge of the Third Reich: the Adam von Trott Memorial Lectures.* Clarendon Press: Oxford.

Melson, R. (1989) Revolutionary genocide: on the causes of the Armenian genocide of 1915 and the Holocaust. *Holocaust and Genocide Studies,* **4,** pp. 161 - 174.

Milgram, S. (1974) *Obedience to Authority.* Tavistock: London

Morris, J. (1979. *Heaven's Command: an imperial progress.* Penguin: Harmondsworth.

Moscovici, S. (1985) *The Age of the Crowd; a historical treatise on mass psychology.* Cambridge University Press: Cambridge

Mugny, G. (1982) *The Power of Minorities.* Academic Press: New York.

Muller-Claudius, M. Cited *in* Cohn, N. (1967).

Perutz, M.F. (1992) The fifth freedom. *New York Review of Books,* Oct 8, pp. 3-7.

Poewe, K. (1985) *The Namibian Herero: a history of their psychosocial disintegration and survival.* Edwin Mellen Press: Lewiston, NY and Queenston,Ontario.

Pol Pot. Cited *in* Carey, P. (1990).

Ponchaud, F. (1978) *Cambodia: Year Zero.* Holt Reinhart and Winston: New York

Pool, G. *Samuel Maherero.* Gamsberg Macmillan: Windhoek.

Reicher, S. (1987) Crowd behaviour as social action. *In* J.C. Turner (ed.). *Rediscovering the Social group.* Blackwell: Oxford.

Riefenstahl, L. (1992) *The Sieve of Time.* Quartet: London.

Ruskin. Cited *in* Morris J. (1979).

Savinkov. Cited *in* Bell, D. (1991).

Shawcross, W. (1986) *Sideshow: Kissinger, Nixon and the destruction of Cambodia.* Hogarth Press: London.

Stachura, D. (1983) *Gregor Strasser and the Rise of Nazism.* George Allen and Unwin: London.

Staub, E. (1989) *The Roots of Evil; the origins of genocide and other group violence.* Cambridge University Press: New York.

Staub, E. (1990) Genocide and mass killing: cultural, societal and psychological origins. *In* Himmelweit, H.T. and Gaskell, G. (eds) *Societal psychology.* SAGE: London pp. 230 - 250.

Strasser, G. Cited *in* Stachura, P. (1983).

Strauss, H.A. (1988) Hostages of "World Jewry": on the origin of the idea of genocide in German history. *Holocaust and Genocide Studies,* **3,** pp. 125 -136.

Tajfel, H. (ed.) (1978) *Differentiation Between Social Groups.* Academic Press: London

Taylor, A.J.P. (1975) The seizure of power. *In* Fertig, H. (ed.) *The Third Reich.* Weidenfeld and Nicholson: London.

Terborgh, J. (1992) A matter of life and death. *New York Review of Books,* November 5, pp. 3 - 6.

Tolstoya, T. (1991) In cannibalistic times. *New York Review of Books,* April 11, pp. 3 - 6.

Tucker, R.C. (1973) *Stalin as Revolutionary.* Norton: New York.

Tucker, R.C. (1987) *Political Culture and Leadership.* Norton: New York.

Tucker, R.C. (1990) *Stalin in Power.* Norton: New York.

Volkogonoff, D. (1991) *Stalin; Triumph and Tragedy.* Weidenfeld and Nicolson: London.

Von Klemperer, K. (1986) Widerstand - Resistance: the place of the German resistance in the European resistance against National Socialism. *In* Bull, H. (ed.) *The Challenge of the Third Reich: the Adam von Trott Memorial Lectures.* Clarendon Press: Oxford, pp. 35 - 56.

Von Schlabrendorff, F. (1965) *The Secret War Against Hitler.* Hodder and Stoughton: London.

Waite, R. (1977) *The Psychopathic God: Adolf Hitler.* Basic Books: New York.

Walker, C.J. (1980) *Armenia: the Survival of a Nation.* Croom Helm: London.

Weber, E. (1988) A new order of profit and loss. *Times Literary Supplement,* Jan 15, pp. 51 - 52.

Weindling, P. (1990) *Health, Race and German Politics Between National Unification and Nazism, 1870 - 1945.* Cambridge University Press: Cambridge.

Xianliang, Z. (1986) *Half of Man is Woman.* Penguin: London.

INDEX

Abel, 42
Action schema, 92
Ahmed, 127
Aid, 57-58, 125
Angka, 61, 63
Apartheid, 10, 74
Arendt, 12, 94
Argentina, 76
Argyll, Duke of, 31
Armenians, 5, 30-35, 82
Authoritarianism, 91

Bangladesh, 8, 25
Baynes, 45, 115, 118
Bengali, 6, 75, 76
Biafran war, 22-27
Bielenberg, 87-89, 110, 117
Binion, 112
Boer War, 18
Bolshevik, 50, 66, 101, 119, 120
Bombing Cambodia, 63
Bonhoeffer, 94
Bosnia, 74
Botswana, 72
Brazil, 8
Broszat, 40
Browning, 86
Bukharin, 53, 118
Burgler, 55
Bushmen, 71-72

Cambodia, 54-64
Carrier, Jean-Baptiste, 54
Chalk, 5, 9, 48
Chandler, 56
China, 6
Choice, 107-110
Church, 98
CIA, 57
Cocks, 112
Cohn, 36, 37
Colonization, 15-17
Columbus, 16
Concentration camps, 18, 50
Conquest, Robert, 50
Constituent Assembly, 50
Culture of genocide, 96-99

De St Jorre, 26
Deutscher, 53
Diversity, 124-125, 135
Djugashvili, 118, 120
Drechsler, 20
Dressen, 98
Du Preez, 108
Duranty, 35, 53

Ecology of genocide, 129-131
Eichmann, 12, 94
El Salvador, 76

Ethnocide, 72
Eugenics, 97

Fein, 68, 71, 76
Fischer, 35, 53
Forsyth, 26
French in Indochina, 56-57
Furtwangler, 86

Gaddafi, 126
Galeano, 105
Games, 85
Gayid, 90
Geneva agreement, 59
Genocide
    activators, 86
    classification of, 68-81
    colonization, 15-21, 68
    decolonization, 22-27, 68
    definition, 7-10, 14-15, 48
    despotic, 68, 76-77
    developmental, 68, 71-73
    hegemonic, 68, 73-75
    ideological, 68, 69
    in antiquity, 4-5
    list of, 5-7, 78-79
    models, 80-82
    movements, 83-85
    potential, 82
    pragmatic, 67, 68, 69
    repressive, 68, 75-76
    retributive, 69, 70-71
    revolutionary, 65-68
    stages, 14
    theory of, 129-132
    transcendent, 11-12
    xenophobic, 69
Ginzberg, 88
Goerdeler, 88
Goering, 112, 133
Gokalp, 33

Group formation, 91, 107
Gross, Dr Walter, 43, 44
Guatemala, 75
Guinea, 75
Gulf war, 127, 132
Gurr, 68, 69, 71, 75, 77, 80
Gypsies 6, 98

Harff, 68, 69, 71, 75, 77, 80, 84
Harkis, 70
Hatuey, 105
Hegel, 65, 70
Herero, 1-2, 5, 11, 15, 17, 19-22
Heyd, 33
Hilberg, 46, 47, 98
Hirst, 89
Hitler, ii, 29, 35-47, 85, 88-89, 101, 112-117
Ho Chi Minh, 56
Hoffmann, 109
Holocaust, 35-47, 81
Hostage groups, 28-29, 126
Hutu, 6, 70

Ibo, 6, 11, 22-27, 75
Ideologeme, 130
Ideologies
    acceleration, 104-107
    hitchhiking, 130
    resistance, 134
    transformation, 103-104, 106
    unpacking, 133
Ieng Sary, 59
India, 7, 76
Indonesia, 6, 7
Intervention, right of, 132
Iraq, 75
Irrationality, 128-129
Ironsi, 24
Islamic Association, 90

Ludlow, 89

Jews, 2-3, 6, 12, 35-47, 86, 115
Jonassohn, 5, 48
Joodsche Raad, 94
Justifications of genocide, 17-19, 24,
32-33, 43-45, 51, 60-61

Mace, 35, 53
Madagascar, 75
Malaya, 75
Mandelstam, 65
Maharero, 19
Kaldun, 128
Martov, 101
Kampuchea, 7, 54-64
Marxism, 49-54, 65, 69
Kano, 25, 27
Mason, 109
Kedourie, 116, 126
Mein Kampf, 29, 39, 43, 98, 114
Kelso, 72
Melson, 81
Kent State, 62
Menshevik, 101, 120
Kerensky, 102
Milgram, 107
Kettenacker, 41
Mobutu, 76
Keystone authorities, 124-125, 131
Morris, 18
Keystone species, 124-125
Moscovici, 108
Khieu Samphan, 60
Movements
Khmer Issarak, 56
    ecology, 100
Khmer Rouge, 6-7, 54-64
    genocidal, 99-102
Khmer Serei, 57
    leadership, 101-102
Kiernan, 59
    range, 100
Klee, 98
    structure, 99
Knodn, 98
Muggeridge, 53
Koba, 119
Mugny, 108
Kulaks, 5, 49-54
Muller-Claudius, 42
Kuper, 9, 68, 71, 132
Multiculturalism, 124, 135
Kurds, 75
Muslim, 74, 75, 124-127

Langer, 112
Namibia, 1, 15-21
Laws,psychological, 93
Naxalites, 76
Leber, 109
Nazis, 2, 35-47, 67, 87-89, 98
Lenin, 48, 101, 118
Nigeria, 11, 22-27, 75
Lemkin, 7
Nihilism, 133
Leuschner, 109
Lewis, 32
OAU, 22
Lewontin, 130
Ottoman, 30-35, 70
Levi-Strauss, 70
Obedience, 91, 107
Lifton, 97
Owerri, 26
Littell, 82-83
Lon Nol, 58, 62
Paine, 124

Pakistan, 8, 75
Paraguay, 8
Perutz, 125
Philippines, 76
Political culture of genocide, 96-99, 118-119
Pluralism, 135
Poewe, 20
Pol Pot, 54, 59, 61, 133
Politicide, 48-49
Ponchaud, 55, 61
Pool, 21
Poverty, 125-126
Power, 92
Prejudice, 91
Protocols - of Learned Elders of Zion, 56, 115
Psychobiography, 111, 112
    Hitler, 112-117
    Stalin, 118-121
Psycho-logic, 29
Psychology of politics, 95-96, 96-121
Purification, 28

Rage, 122-124
Rationality, 3-4, 128-129
Redistribution,122-124
Reicher, 93
Reductionism, 104
Resistance in Germany, 108-110
Revolution, 65-68
Riefenstahl, 117
Riess, 98
Right
    of discovery, 2, 16
    to vacant land,2, 16
Russo-Turkish war, 30
Ruskin, 18

Sacrifice groups, 28-29
Saddam, 12, 127

Sassun, 31
Savinkov, 103
SEATO, 57
Serbs, 7, 74
Science of genocide, 85
Shawcross, 55, 59
Sihanouk, 57, 62
Slavs, 98
Social ecology, 129-132
Social psychology
    minimalist, 90-92
    of politics, 95-96, 92-121
South Africa, 10, 74
South Vietnamese, 62
Speer, 117
Stalin, ii, 35, 51-54, 118-121
Stauffenberg, 108, 109
Staub, 97
Steiner, George, 70
Strasser, Gregor, 28
Strategic approach, 93-95, 129-132
Strauss, 98
Sudan, 75
Superpowers, 57, 64
Susceptiblity to genocidal ideas, 127, 130, 133

Tajfel, 107
Talaat Pasha, 35
Tamil, 70
Taylor A.J.P., 38, 39, 41, 65
Tecklenberg, 21
Terborgh, 125
Timor, 2, 7
Tolstoya, 49
Trapp, 87
Trebizond, 31
Tucker, 118, 119, 120
Turks, 30-35
Tutsi, 6

Typology of genocides
      analysis, 68-81
      table, 78-79

Ukraine, 75
United Nations, 8-10, 55-56, 64
United States, 8, 57, 62, 63
Utopians, 105-107, 126

Versailles treaty, 38, 108
Violent conflict, 9
Volkogonoff, 52, 53, 118, 119
Von Klemperer, 94
Von Moltke, 110
Von Reichenau, 99
Von Schlabrendorff, 133, 134
Von Trotha, 2, 20
Von Trott, 110
Vichy France, 56

Waite, 112, 114
Walker, 30, 35
Waterberg, 20-21
Weindling, 97
Wilson Government in UK, 26

Xianling, 105

Yugoslavia, 73-74

Zaire, 76

Also available in the *Briefing*s Series

Before the Beginning is a radical attempt to explain and redefine the origins and purpose of creation. Professor Ellis deals clearly and authoritatively with new scientific theories explaining how things began and elucidates the laws which control the operation of the universe. In addition he describes the complex mechanism by which the laws of physics appear to govern and facilitate, as well as to sustain human life. His conclusions about the very meaning of life are often unexpected, but the process by which he reaches them is illuminating and scientifically sound, as would be expected from one of the world's foremost cosmologists.

George Ellis is Professor of Cosmic Physics at SISSA in Trieste, Italy and Professor of Applied Mathematics at the University of Cape Town, South Africa. A former Fellow of Peterhouse, Cambridge, he is GC Macvittie Visiting Professor of Astronomy in the School of Mathematics at Queen Mary and Westfield College, London University. Amongst his many publications, he is the author, jointly with Stephen Hawking, of *The Large Scale Structure of Space-Time*.

ISBN 0 7145 2970 2

Ideology After the Fall of Communism looks at the likely developments in ideological thinking after the fall of the Berlin Wall in 1989. Will one particular brand of political philosophy come to dominate world thinking now that Soviet Communism is no longer a force to be reckoned with? If so, will it be liberal democracy - the system prevailing in the USA and the EEC? Or will some other kind of irresistible movement sweep all before it - nationalism, religious fundamentalism, market forces raw in tooth and claw, or some form of non-Marxian socialism? The author explores all these possibilities and offers his own bold and controversial predictions.

Peter Collins - Editor of *Briefings* - gained first class honours in Philosophy at London University. He now teaches Political Philosophy in the University of Cape Town's Department of Political Studies, where he is presently Senior Lecturer.

ISBN 0 7145 2971 0